Break To Breakthrough

Career revival roadmap for mothers

Break To Breakthrough

Career revival roadmap for mothers

Shreeja Kurup Anil

Highbrow Scribes Publications
New Delhi

Break To Breakthrough
Career revival roadmap for mothers

Published 2024 by Highbrow Scribes Publications

Printed in New Delhi, India

ISBN: 978-81-969209-7-5

Highbrow Scribes Publications's mission is to foster a universal passion for reading by partnering with authors to help create stories and communicate ideas that inform, entertain, and inspire, and to connect them with readers everywhere.

Highbrow Scribes Publications books are printed on acid-free paper.

www.highbrowscribes.com

Dedication

For women aiming to break free from their current reality and embark on a new path

Contents

Note from Author

Dear Reader,

I hope this note finds you well, fill you up with the excitement of possibilities and get you ready to embark on a remarkable journey. As an entrepreneur and mentor, I have experienced firsthand the transformative power of embracing change and starting anew.

Life is an ever-changing tapestry of experiences, and every new chapter offers us a chance to redefine ourselves, our goals, and our aspirations. Embrace the notion that it's okay to restart; in fact, it's more than okay, it's courageous! Recognize that you possess the strength to adapt, learn, and grow from any challenges that come your way.

Creating a new path demands self-awareness. Take the time to understand your passions, values, and unique strengths. Remember, the most fulfilling ventures are often born from the intersection of your skills and your deepest desires. Don't be afraid to explore uncharted territories and discover untapped potential within yourself.

While charting your new course, expect setbacks and failures. These are not signs of defeat but stepping stones towards growth and resilience that propel you towards growth. Embrace them with an open mind, as they offer valuable lessons that will shape your journey in unexpected ways.

Surround yourself with a supportive network of like-minded individuals. Seek mentors, peers, and collaborators who share your vision and can offer guidance during moments of doubt. Remember, seeking support is not a sign of weakness but a sign of wisdom.

Flexibility is key in the ever-changing landscape of entrepreneurship. Be prepared to adapt your plans and strategies as needed. Embrace innovation and continuous learning, for it is through curiosity and an open mind that breakthroughs are born.

As you embark on this new path journey, remember that success is not solely defined by external achievements, but also by the growth and evolution you experience along the way. Celebrate every milestone, no matter how small, use them as fuel to drive you forward.

Lastly, stay true to your purpose. Define your mission, and let it be the guiding force behind your decisions and actions. As you create your new path, let your passion, perseverance, and determination be your guiding compass.

Know that I believe in you wholeheartedly and stand ready to support you in any way I can. This journey will be filled with ups and downs, but I am confident that the strength and brilliance you carry within will lead you to great heights. May this new path be one of growth, fulfillment, and purpose. Embrace it with open arms, for the possibilities are endless.

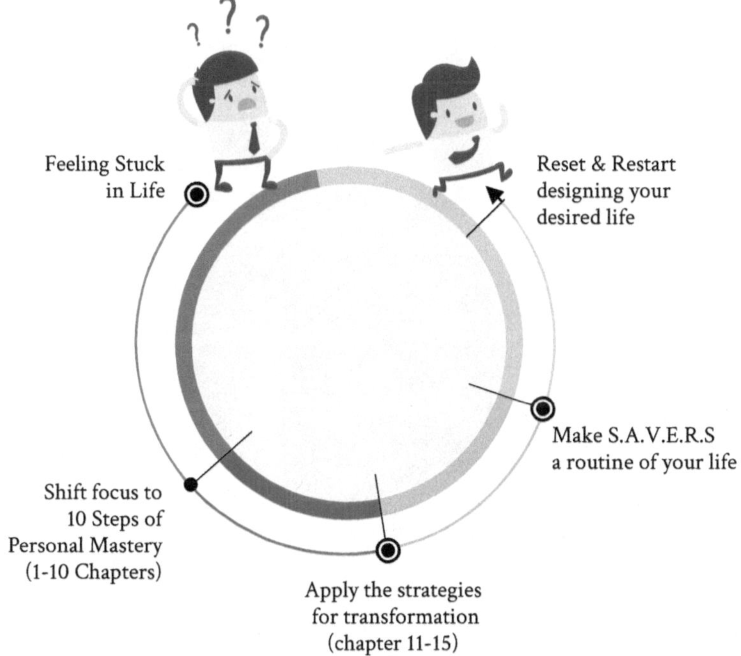
? ? ?
Feeling Stuck
in Life
Reset & Restart
designing your
desired life
Make S.A.V.E.R.S
a routine of your life
Shift focus to
10 Steps of
Personal Mastery
(1-10 Chapters)
Apply the strategies
for transformation
(chapter 11-15)

Introduction

Into an abyss I shrank

I was back to zero, despite being at the pinnacle of success in my career, when I decided to call it quits. I was all of 35.

I didn't know when days turned into nights and months as I struggled to stay afloat to play the roles I couldn't outsource - a wife, a daughter, a sister, a friend and most importantly a mother!

Neither could I recognize the face I saw in the mirror nor could I remember the feeling in my heart. All I heard was the chatter in my mind that grew insanely louder echoing the noises of family, society and the world at large.

Two years after a major surgery a happy moment came into our lives - elated and excited, we were looking forward to our new blessing. My health was not up to the mark, complications of the surgery had weakened my body and my emotions, I kept telling myself I am strong and I can manage, but the truth was far from it. Work was at its busiest; holding a senior position meant responsibilities. I expected my team and colleagues to help me go through this phase. Sadly, that was not to be.

The months following the first term proved more challenging, beyond my ability to cope. The persistent stress at work and ongoing mental and physical strain exacerbated my health issues. My doctor issued a health warning because of gestational diabetes, leading to dietary restrictions. I had to monitor my glucose levels by pricking myself three times a day and recording the results. I was not sure why was all this happening and one other person who was affected by this was my 5-year-old son. Every time I looked at him, I felt more sad and my heart ached. I used to ask why this is happening to me, and to God I started praying harder. I was always sad and unhappy, when that was the time, I should have been happy and relaxed. The last trimester was terrible. Unable to find comfort in sleep, I resorted to resting in a seated position with pillows providing support to my back. I was advised bedrest for last month before the due date. The events after that broke me completely. I was denied leave from work stating year-end issues. When I insisted, I had to hear comments like 'she is lazy, just making health an issue'; 'pregnancy is a good excuse for women to rest full time and enjoy long work leave that too paid.' One of the worst was that 'women are taking space of men and enjoying all perks, getting rest and money while men have to just work harder with no privileges', etc.

Following an emergency surgery, my daughter came much earlier than expected. By the grace of God and all my elders' blessings, she survived some difficult days giving me a ray of hope to hang on in life. I mentally prepared to tackle life with a fresh start, but thought of joining work made me anxious. At this time, I yearned to have someone whom I could talk to and discuss the professional difficulties I faced, someone who could guide me on how to deal with these people especially after knowing their intensions and thoughts. It was disheartening for me to be in the same place as them.

I resumed work 45 days after giving birth. All my buildup strength was blown to fragments as my senior denied feeding time granted to new mothers, saying that I was in a senior position and there was no replacement available. A colleague had gone on vacation the day I joined without handing over or as much as briefing me of what happened in my absence. His reason was I had rest during my delivery leave and it was time he took some rest!! Not only were his responsibilities given to me, two other senior male members present were ordered not to share my workload. I requested, for the sake of my daughter's health, to allow me just one month for feeding time, but she refused.

The fact that she had a 2-year-old child and she was still availing feeding hour relief while refusing to give me at least a month's time hurt me. I expected at least a woman to understand my situation. Listening to the pinching words of colleagues coupled with this behavior from my senior I began to lose interest; I was not able to contribute at work.

At the time I had no clue what I would do; staying in the UAE without a job would affect my visa status and with one income, home finances would be stretched. And to top it all, banking was not just a profession for me. Years ago, as a young girl, I had visited a bank in India with my father. There I saw the operations head, a beautiful lady, so graceful. What impressed me was the respect she was getting from everyone around; that image imprinted on my mind, and banking became my only choice of career. I became curious about finance, savings and investments.

I majored in Finance and came to the UAE in 2004 and started my career with one of the leading banks. I was excited to learn about international banking along with trade finance, i.e., international import and export. The more I learned the more possibilities and opportunities opened up before me. I enjoyed the speed of my career growth and built big dreams. Life was good; everything seemed perfect. Professionally that was the best phase I was in.

Therefore, the decision I took was the most difficult one. After numerous sleepless nights and panic attacks, I made the much-dreaded move – I quit the high-paying job of more than 15 years. I announced to family and friends that I am on a sabbatical to recapture my life (which was lost somewhere in between kids, banking and no direction).

If I anticipated a smooth journey, where everything would effortlessly fall into place, and I could seamlessly rejoin the workforce or revive my professional path after sorting out my life, I would be painfully mistaken. My decision had unleashed the proverbial Pandora's box, and I found myself engulfed in emotional and mental anguish, grappling with societal expectations, familial pressures, ingrained conditioning, pervasive myths, and stifling orthodoxy. I was called crazy by one and all. Only my husband stood with me without asking a question. He is my strength to date!

I needed to fix myself for the two beautiful souls that I am responsible for, more than anything or anyone in this life. I had no guide or help on how to move forward, but I was determined to carve my path. I wanted to create my own identity, and that was easier said than done, because the woman I was could not understand the woman I wanted to become. She was mired beneath layers of conditioning, fears and prejudices.

I realized that I was a woman who sought comfort in every aspect of life; who was scared of change and uncertainty; who avoided situations that made me uncomfortable and felt under confident and fragile.

My pain, however, transcended the personal; it was a poignant reflection of the challenges mothers face when daring to take a sabbatical, hoping to rediscover and redefine themselves in a world that often misunderstands or underestimates their transformative journey. According to a study by the World Bank, 20 million Indian women quit jobs between 2004-'12. Around 65-70% of women who quit did not return to work at all. In India, women account for 25 percent of the workforce and, according to a report by the Indian Women Network, 36 percent of them take a break from work.

I could have effortlessly fallen into this category had I not deliberately made the effort to resurrect myself, as the ramifications of taking a sabbatical are manifold.

Practical challenges loomed large, including strained relationships. Navigating personal and professional ties became a delicate balancing act. Financial stability, once a given, morphed into a precarious concern.

Emotionally, I grappled with guilt and struggled to manage anger issues. The internal conflict intensified as societal expectations clashed with my pursuit of personal growth. Guilt, an unwelcome companion, constantly whispered doubts about my decision to prioritize self-discovery.

Mentally, I confronted the daunting impostor syndrome. The hiatus from the structured corporate world plunged me into uncharted territory, where self-doubt threatened to overshadow any new move I decided to make. The struggle to reconcile my evolving identity with established norms fueled the mental challenges, casting shadows on the journey of self-resurrection.

I was in such an abyss, when I came across a video from a mindfulness coach, introducing me to the term 'Mindfulness'. This was in 2014. Learning and understanding mindfulness gave me a lot of clarity. Focus on life shifted to a conscious choice of living - more understanding of what I want and what is of no use to me. My perception of life shifted to my happiness and my family's happiness rather than only accumulation of materials and building wealth. Meditation and journaling became a part of my life, most important of all I learned to heal my old wounds and slowly the scars of the past started fading away. Priority of life became health and personal growth. The positivity in my life began to reflect in my children's life as well. I get to hear their praises at parent-teacher meetings, which gives me so much happiness and pride.

Today, as the self-empowerment learnings continue, I have started on my entrepreneurial journey. I am confident and at peace, both personally and professionally. And I wish the same for any mother unhappy with her life.

I've distilled all my mistakes, learnings, trials and errors so as to spare you the arduous path I navigated. I have created a threefold-blueprint for breaking free from a stagnant life and welcoming peace, joy, and prosperity with empowerment and contentment. It revolves around Personal Mastery, Purpose, and Powerful Planning. In the upcoming chapters, we'll delve into these strategies.

Happy reading and self-reflection!

Personal Mastery

Though it took time and many efforts to stick to learning and practicing mindfulness, with continuous efforts focusing on the present moment started becoming easier since those pathways were getting used routinely. Through mindfulness I was able to acknowledge my thoughts, better understand the thought patterns and accept them without emotions. When we take time to focus on our thoughts and are conscious of our mind, we begin to "rewire" our brain. By consciously being aware of our thoughts in the present moment, we strengthen those neuron connections that are being used.

Learning to be mindful completely changed how I lived. It made me care about myself again, taking care of all aspects of who I am. I felt my anxiety and depression loosen their hold on me, allowing me to start living again. And finally, after over a chaotic decade of self-deception and self-hate, I found myself reclaiming my freedom, my mind, and my life.

Going through these stages of clarity can also bring up old pain and remind us of our past. This helps us understand why we experienced certain things. My own journey in my career is a good example of this. From a young age, we're taught to compare ourselves to others and to compete. This idea is ingrained in us at school, within our families, and in our communities. We often feel pressure to meet other people's expectations and choose our paths based on the need to prove ourselves successful and better than others.

I had chosen Banking because I liked it, I enjoyed it, too, but something changed when responsibilities increased and so did the competition, the feeling of, "I lack or I do not deserve" set in. Had I known the things I know today I would have changed the course of my journey. Now I understand that it was because I was not aligned with what I wanted and had created an imbalance which I was not able to handle. That is where personal mastery stepped into my life.

In order to take control of developing a sense of who you are, what you can do, where you are going coupled with the ability to influence your communication, emotions, and behavior on the way to getting there, you have to be connected to yourself first.

Why is it important to cultivate Personal Mastery?

Cultivating Personal Mastery is important for various reasons, as it contributes to individual well-being, personal development, and success in different aspects of life. Here are several reasons why cultivating Personal Mastery is considered valuable:

Growth and Development: Personal Mastery encourages a mindset of continuous learning and growth. It helps individuals expand their skills, knowledge, and capacities throughout their lives.

Adaptability in a changing world: In today's rapidly changing world, adaptability is crucial. Personal mastery fosters the ability to adapt to new circumstances, navigate uncertainties, and thrive in changing environments.

Self-Awareness: Developing personal mastery involves gaining a deeper understanding of oneself, including strengths, weaknesses, values, and motivations. This heightened self-awareness can lead to better decision-making and improved relationships.

Problem-Solving Skills: Critical thinking and creativity contribute to improved problem-solving abilities. Individuals who cultivate personal mastery are often better equipped to find innovative solutions to challenges.

Improved Resilience: Builds resilience by teaching them how to bounce back from setbacks and learn from failures. This resilience is valuable in facing life's inevitable ups and downs.

Effective Communication: It also includes the development of effective communication skills, which are essential in building positive relationships, collaborating with others, and fostering a supportive social network.

Leadership Skills: Leaders who cultivate personal mastery often exhibit qualities such as vision, integrity, and effective communication. These attributes contribute to successful leadership and inspire others to follow.

Grater Satisfaction and Fulfillment: As individuals align their actions with their values and work towards meaningful goals, they are likely to experience a greater sense of satisfaction and fulfillment in their lives.

Positive Impact on Health and Well-being: Personal Mastery is associated with well-being and a positive mindset. Stress management, self-care, and a balanced lifestyle are often integral aspects contributing to overall health.

Cultivating and practicing Personal Mastery allows individuals to live authentically and contribute positively to their communities. This can lead to the creation of a meaningful legacy that extends beyond personal accomplishments. It equips individuals with the skills and mindset needed to navigate life's challenges successfully and lead fulfilling, purpose-driven lives.

There are five key aspects of life that have the most significant impact on us and require mastery to enhance our growth and success. They are:

1. **Health** - Taking care of your health is the most important thing in life. It helps you control your body, mind, and emotions. When these are balanced, you not only look good but also feel good. And when you look and feel good, you attract good things into your life.
2. **Mindset** - Your mindset is a set of beliefs that shape how you make sense of the world and yourself. It influences how you think, feel, and behave in any given situation. It means that what you believe about yourself will impact your success or failure.
3. **Relationship** - Mastering this skill will help you connect deeply with others and feel the rewarding sense of contributing to their lives, making a difference.
4. **Finance** - This teaches you to thrive, not just survive, in your prime years and beyond. Living in a capitalist society means we all have the chance to pursue our dreams.
5. **Time management** - Here you will see how short-term evaluations can prevent long-term problems. Then, you'll figure out how to plan and execute your decisions effectively. Once you've mastered time, you'll realize that people often think they can do more in a year and less in a decade than they actually can!

Personal Mastery goes beyond competence and skill. It means approaching one's life as a creative work of art, living life from a creative point as opposed to a reactive viewpoint. Personal Mastery is when you become your own guiding light. It is the process where you strive to become the better version of your own self.

There are different definitions of Personal Mastery. However, there is a need to understand that it is not about the destination but the process of nurturing and evolving. We can witness a positive change in our personal as well as professional life if we choose to be a part of this journey. Understanding our thoughts, vision, and what we are, is an essential aspect of Personal Mastery.

Successful entrepreneurs have a clear mindset of what they want and how they can achieve their goals. They are aware of the fact that if they have to lead a strong team, they need to lead themselves properly. So, they prioritize Personal Mastery.

Personal Mastery is like a toolkit that helps you be more creative, achieve high-quality results, and reach your full potential. It's about being the best version of yourself and carrying yourself with grace, without feeling the need to compete with others. Many people have goals, but sometimes they get sidetracked by other things along the way. Those who focus on personal growth know themselves well and what they want in life. They don't just focus on one thing; they can look at different aspects of their life and make decisions that help them achieve their goals. Personal Mastery helps you identify your habits, emotions, and behaviors that influence your decision-making, which is crucial for running a successful business or achieving any goal.

Components of Personal Mastery

Personal Mastery involves various components aimed at continuous self-improvement and development. Some key components commonly that guided me on my path include…

Self-Awareness: Understanding one's strengths, weaknesses, values, beliefs, and emotions. Self-awareness is the foundation of Personal Mastery.

Clarity of Vision: Having a clear sense of purpose, values, and long-term vision for one's life will help in decision-making and actions, aligning them with personal goals and aspirations.

Goal Setting: Establishing specific, measurable, achievable, relevant, and time-bound (SMART) goals will help set clear objectives providing direction and motivation for personal development.

Identifying Mindset: A commitment to lifelong learning and a growth mindset. Embracing new knowledge and skills enable individuals to adapt to changing circumstances and stay relevant in their personal and professional lives.

Effective Communication: Developing strong communication skills to express ideas clearly, listen actively, and build positive relationships with others is crucial for collaboration and teamwork.

Focus: Regularly reflecting on experiences, actions, and outcomes and focusing on enhancement of self-awareness will help in learning from successes and failures.

Building Habits: Much of what we do every day is automatic - habits we might not even notice whether good or bad. We can use this to our advantage by identifying which habits will benefit us the most and intentionally developing them.

Spirituality and Mindfulness: Developing a sense of spirituality or mindfulness practices will help in finding inner peace, reflecting on yourself, and feeling more connected to both you and the world around you.

Time Management: Efficiently allocating time to tasks and priorities. Time management skills are essential for maintaining a balance between personal and professional responsibilities.

Self-Regulation: Exercising self-control and discipline in managing one's behavior, emotions, and reactions. Self-regulation contributes to maintaining composure and making rational decisions.

These components work together synergistically, contributing to an individual's overall Personal Mastery. Cultivating these aspects can lead to a more fulfilling and purposeful life while facilitating continuous growth and development. In the next chapters we will see how these components are helpful in personal development and growth.

How Personal Mastery will help women on a sabbatical to get back to work

Personal Mastery can play a significant role in helping women on a sabbatical to successfully re-enter the workforce. It is continuous improvement and development of oneself, both personally and professionally. Here are several ways in which Personal Mastery can benefit women returning to work after a sabbatical.

Skill Development: During a sabbatical, women may have the opportunity to acquire new skills or enhance existing ones. Personal Mastery encourages ongoing learning and skill development, which can make them more competitive in the job market.

Confidence Building: Women who have taken a break from their careers may experience a lack of confidence. Engaging in Personal Mastery practices, such as setting and achieving personal goals, can help boost confidence, making it easier to transition back to the workforce.

Adaptability and Resilience: The job market and workplace dynamics can change during a sabbatical. Personal Mastery practices can help develop adaptability and resilience, crucial qualities when re-entering the workforce.

Networking and Relationship Building: These skills are essential for networking, which is crucial for re-entering the workforce. Building a strong professional network can provide support, mentorship, and potential job opportunities.

Goal Setting and Planning: Women on a sabbatical may have had time to reassess their career goals and aspirations. Personal Mastery involves setting clear goals and creating a plan to achieve them, helping women gain a clear direction and purpose.

Flexibility and Open-Mindedness: Women returning to work after a sabbatical may encounter changes in the industry or workplace. Personal Mastery fosters open-mindedness and flexibility.

Time Management and Prioritization: Balancing personal and professional commitments is a skill developed through Personal Mastery, which will stand women returning to work in good stead.

1

Self-Awareness Foundation of Personal Mastery - Significance of Self-Awareness

"Knowing yourself is the beginning of all wisdom. Self-Awareness is the key to self-mastery."

In both my work and personal life, I used to handle situations as they came, without much thought or awareness. This often led to stress, chaos, and missed opportunities. Personal Mastery is about always improving and growing, and a big part of that is being self-aware. This chapter explains how understanding yourself deeply is essential for personal growth, and how it forms the foundation for becoming better overall.

Self-awareness means understanding your thoughts, feelings, actions, strengths, weaknesses, values, and motivations. It's not just recognizing surface-level stuff but delving deep into what makes you, YOU. When you're self-aware, you can see yourself clearly, manage your feelings, act in line with your values, and grasp how others see you, as well as how you see yourself.

Simply put, highly self-aware people can accurately understand why they do what they do, how they feel, and what they think. It's a rare skill because many of us get caught up in our emotions and interpretations of situations, just like I did. Developing self-awareness is crucial because it helps leaders assess their progress, make changes when needed, and understand themselves better.

Self-awareness isn't something you're hyper-focused on all the time. Instead, it becomes a natural part of who you are, showing up at different times depending on the situation and your personality.

Why is self-awareness important

Self-awareness and self-love are interconnected aspects of personal development that contribute to overall well-being. Understanding and embracing who you are, along with cultivating a positive and compassionate attitude toward yourself, creating a powerful synergy for personal growth. Here's how self-awareness and self-love are intertwined:

Understanding Your Needs: Self-awareness helps in identifying emotional, physical, and psychological needs. Recognizing these needs is a crucial first step toward fulfilling them and promoting self-love.

Acknowledging Strengths and Weaknesses: Gaining a realistic understanding of your strengths and weaknesses, embracing both aspects without judgment fosters self-love by allowing you to appreciate our abilities while acknowledging areas for improvement.

Acceptance of Imperfections: Encourages acceptance of your imperfections and quirks. Instead of dwelling on perceived flaws, you learn to embrace them as unique aspects of your identity, fostering self-love.

Mindful Self-Compassion: Involves recognizing moments of self-criticism or negative self-talk and pivoting them with self-love, you can practice mindful self-compassion, treating yourself with the same kindness you would offer a friend during challenging times.

Clarifying Personal Values: By identifying and clarifying your personal values. Aligning your actions and decisions with these values contributes to a sense of purpose and fulfillment, nurturing self-love.

Nurturing Healthy Relationships: Being self-aware helps you understand the type of relationships that align with your values. Eliminating unaligned relationships and engaging in positive, respectful relationships contributes to a supportive environment for self-love to thrive.

Having a solid understanding of yourself is like building a strong base. Self-love means accepting, nurturing, and looking after the person you've come to know through self-awareness. When these two work together, they create a powerful force for personal growth, resilience, and forming better relationships with yourself and others.

Self-awareness can be a powerful catalyst for women looking to restart their lives after a break. Whether the break was due to personal reasons, career shifts, family responsibilities, or any other circumstances, cultivating self-awareness can help women navigate this transitional phase with clarity and purpose.

Enables women to identify their core values and priorities. Understanding what truly matters to them helps in making decisions aligned with their authentic selves as they embark on restarting their lives. Through self-awareness, women can gain clarity on their goals and aspirations. This involves defining both short-term and long-term objectives, creating a roadmap for the desired life they want to build.

Recognizing personal strengths and skills is vital in leveraging one's capabilities. Self-awareness allows women to assess their competencies, empowering them to explore opportunities that align with their abilities. Understanding and acknowledging areas for growth and improvement. Embracing a growth mindset allows women to view challenges as opportunities for learning and development, contributing to a more resilient mindset.

Women restarting their lives often encounter changes and transitions. Self-awareness fosters adaptability, helping them navigate uncertainties and embrace the evolving nature of life with resilience and openness. Knowing oneself includes recognizing the need for support. Women can use self-awareness to build a strong support system, including friends, family, mentors, or communities that align with their values and aspirations.

Self-awareness encourages women to explore their passions and interests. Whether it's a career shift, pursuing a hobby, or engaging in community service, aligning life choices with personal interests contributes to a more fulfilling life. It Is like having a map for your journey, making it easier to navigate. Women can create their own customized plan, which might involve learning new skills, pursuing further education, or taking part in activities that help them grow and feel fulfilled.

Self-awareness serves as a guiding light for women seeking to restart their lives. By understanding themselves deeply, women can make intentional choices, set meaningful goals, achieve greater success and navigate transitions with resilience, ultimately working towards creating the desired and fulfilling life they envision.

Practical Steps for Women Restarting Careers:

- **Self-Assessment:** Conduct a thorough self-assessment to identify skills, strengths, interests, and values.
- **Research and Industry Trends:** Stay informed about industry trends and requirements to align skills with market needs.
- **Update Resumes and Online Profiles:** Tailor

resumes and online profiles to showcase relevant skills and experiences.

- **Networking:** Attend industry events, join professional networks, and connect with professionals in the desired field.
- **Seek Guidance:** Consult with career counsellors, mentors, or professionals who can provide valuable advice.
- **Skill Development:** Identify and address any skill gaps through training programs or certifications.
- **Consider Flexible Work Arrangements:** Explore flexible work options such as part-time, remote work, or freelancing.
- **Job Search Strategies:** Develop a targeted job search strategy, utilizing online job platforms, company websites, and networking.
- **Prepare for Interviews:** Practice common interview questions, showcasing how skills and experiences align with the desired role.
- **Confidence-Building:** Build confidence through positive affirmations, recognizing past achievements, and focusing on strengths.
- **Balance Personal and Professional Goals:** Establish a realistic balance between personal and professional goals to avoid burnout.
- **Stay Resilient:** Understand that the journey may involve setbacks; stay resilient and learn from challenges.

By combining self-awareness with practical strategies, women can navigate their career restart successfully. The mirror within acts as a guide, helping them align their aspirations, skills, and values with their professional pursuits. It's about recognizing one's potential, setting intentional goals, and taking steps to achieve a fulfilling and rewarding career after a break.

Informed Decision-Making

Being self-aware helps you make intentional decisions. When you know your values and priorities, you can make choices that match your long-term goals, leading to a more purposeful life. It's a decision you make after gathering all the relevant information. This means analyzing the potential results, benefits, and risks of each option, and then choosing the one that best fits your needs and moves you closer to your goals

Making informed decisions is crucial for several reasons. Firstly, it instills confidence in your choices and helps prevent doubts afterward. Secondly, it enables you to understand the risks and benefits associated with each option, providing a more realistic outlook on potential outcomes. Additionally, gathering information for informed decision-making may introduce new options that you hadn't previously considered. Ultimately, this approach gives you more control over your choices by taking into account all relevant factors.

Tips to help make informed decisions:

1. **Develop a Mindset for Uncertainties:** The first step in the decision-making process is to acknowledge uncertainties. Knowing that the plan is not foolproof and that there may be setbacks is half the battle won. The right mindset will help you tackle setbacks or failures. If the plan is unsuccessful, you'll be strong enough to treat it as a learning opportunity.
2. **Determine the issue:** First, determine the issue that the informed decision can solve. Identify the aspects of your life that you want to change or problems you want to solve by making a decision. To identify

the issue, ask yourself which option can help you achieve your goals and what obstacles relate to each decision.

3. **Gather data:** Once you identify the issue, begin gathering information that can help you make an informed decision. Ask questions that can offer you more insight into each decision. Here are some questions that you can ask yourself and others to find more information:

   How does this change affect me?

   What is my intuition?

   Does this decision impact my short-term and long-term goals?

   What are my specific options?

   What are the negative effects of each option?

   Is this the right time to make the decision?

4. **Research your options:** Conduct research to grasp the potential outcomes of each decision. Utilize resources such as market research, academic studies, or articles from people facing similar challenges. This research aids in analyzing all potential consequences of your decision.

5. **Consider the outcomes:** After researching, evaluate the outcomes of each decision. Compare the pros and cons of each option to determine the best choice. You can list the advantages and disadvantages of each decision and compare them to decide which option is optimal.

6. **Make a decision:** Analyze the pros and cons of each option before making your decision. Consider all relevant research and questions. Have a colleague or friend who can provide valuable feedback and support during the decision-making process.

7. **Take ownership of your decisions:** Have faith in your abilities and trust your judgment. You've considered everything carefully before making a decision and reminding yourself of your effort can be truly uplifting. Rather than worrying about the outcome, try to focus on perfecting each step in the process.

Authentic Leadership

In the realm of Personal Mastery, authentic leadership is a key outcome of self-awareness. Leaders who are in tune with their values, principles, and emotions inspire trust and respect. They lead by example, creating an environment conducive to collective growth and success.

Authentic leadership is a type of management style in which people act in a real, genuine and sincere way that is true to who they are as individuals. Proponents of authentic leadership say this type of leader is best positioned to inspire trust, loyalty and strong performance

The reason authentic leadership is so important

When we let our emotions run wild, we lose control. We become impulsive, irrational, and sometimes even downright crazy. But when we learn how to harness our emotions for positive change, we gain self-control and make better decisions.

Most of us are taught to suppress our feelings because we're afraid we won't be liked if we show them. This fear often prevents us from expressing ourselves authentically. So, we keep our thoughts bottled up inside, which results in emotional instability and poor decision-making.

But as leaders, we need to recognize our emotions and those of our team members. We need to be able to identify them to lead effectively. If we cannot manage our emotions well, we cannot lead effectively.

Authentic leadership requires three key elements: **Authenticity, Empathy, and Vulnerability.**

Authenticity means showing others our real selves—our true feelings, values, beliefs, hopes, dreams, fears, and attitudes.

Empathy means understanding others' perspectives and experiences.

Vulnerability means sharing our weaknesses with others.

Without these essential qualities, we cannot connect with others and motivate them.

To become an authentic leader, we must practice authenticity, which means being true to ourselves. This helps us feel more secure and confident because we can express our true feelings without fear of rejection. Practicing authenticity allows us to move past fear and anxiety and develop greater confidence and compassion towards others.

In addition to authenticity, empathy is crucial. Empathy involves putting ourselves in others' shoes and asking questions like "How would I feel if I were in their situation?" and "How can I help them?" This helps us understand others' feelings and motivations. When we care about others, we're more likely to act in ways that benefit them..

Resilience and Adaptability

Resilience and adaptability are key qualities for navigating challenges. Resilient individuals have the strength to bounce back from setbacks and can adjust to new situations. Understanding one's own coping mechanisms helps develop effective strategies to tackle obstacles.

Adaptability involves making deliberate choices and navigating changes purposefully. Resilience enables quick recovery from difficulties and allows individuals to move forward with new insights. Adaptation refers to changing to thrive in a new environment, while resilience is the ability to anticipate and cope with shocks, recovering efficiently.

Why adaptability is crucial

Adaptability isn't just about survival; it's also about living a fulfilling life. It enables us to stay calm and focused on unfamiliar situations, find fulfilling careers despite challenges, and navigate parenthood even when overwhelmed. Additionally, adaptability fosters innovation and personal growth, helping us adjust during crises and become better individuals. It teaches humility by showing that despite our plans, we can't always predict outcomes, reminding us of our resilience in the face of uncertainty.

Why resilience is crucial

Resilience is vital in life for numerous reasons. It helps individuals confront obstacles, cope with stress, and devise effective strategies for overcoming difficulties. Additionally, resilience cultivates a positive mindset, mitigating the effects of prolonged stress and emotional strain. It also lowers the risk of mental health issues like anxiety and depression, facilitating recovery from such challenges. Resilient individuals can objectively analyze situations, find solutions, and take proactive steps to address issues, benefiting both personal and professional life. Moreover, resilience fosters empathy, positive connections with others, and the ability to bounce back from failures and learn from setbacks. Overall, resilience enhances well-being by reducing stress, promoting healthier lifestyles, and bolstering the immune system, empowering individuals to navigate life's challenges with strength, adaptability, and optimism, fostering personal growth.

How to cultivate Resilience and Adaptability

Self-awareness: Understanding your strengths and weaknesses is key to building resilience and adaptability.

Continuous Learning: Embrace lifelong learning to stay ahead of the curve and adapt to new situations.

Build a Support Network: Surround yourself with people who can provide guidance, support, and constructive feedback.

Mindfulness and Well-being: Take care of your physical and mental health to maintain a strong foundation for resilience.

Embrace Change: Instead of fearing change, view it as an opportunity for growth.

2

Clarity of Vision - Illuminating the Path Forward

"The strength clarity of your vision will lift you out of the depth of any hardship." **- Robin Sharma**

Standing at life's crossroads, feeling overwhelmed, I found solace in Clarity of Vision. It became my guiding light, leading me out of confusion towards a clearer path. As I embraced this transformative journey, I realized the power of having a clear vision in breaking free from stagnation and finding my true direction. Life had become a monotonous cycle, leaving me entangled in indecision and confusion. The absence of direction fueled unease, prompting me to question my purpose and passions. The necessity for change became evident, and in that darkness, clarity emerged as a beacon of hope, illuminating the way forward.

Why having a clear vision in life is important?

Having a clear vision in life is crucial for several reasons, as it provides direction, purpose, and motivation. Here are some key reasons why having a clear vision is important:

Guidance and Direction: A clear vision serves as a compass, guiding us in our journey through life. It provides a sense of direction, helping us make decisions and choose paths that align with our long-term goals and aspirations.

Motivation and Inspiration: A compelling vision acts as a source of motivation. It gives us a reason to wake up each day with enthusiasm and determination, as we are working towards something meaningful and inspiring.

Focus and Prioritization: With a clear vision, we can channel our energy towards what truly matters. It helps us prioritize tasks and decisions based on long-term goals, avoiding distractions and unnecessary diversions.

Overcoming Challenges: A clear vision acts as a source of resilience in difficult times. It motivates us to overcome obstacles, as we can see beyond immediate hardships and stay focused on our ultimate objectives.

Personal Growth and Development: A clear vision fosters continuous personal growth. It challenges us to acquire new skills, expand our knowledge, and evolve as we pursue our vision. This dedication to growth leads to a more fulfilling and enriched life.

Increased Self-Confidence: Knowing our direction and having faith in our chosen path boosts self-assurance, enabling us to confront challenges with optimism.

Alignment of Values: A clear vision enables us to align our actions with our core values, fostering authenticity and integrity in our choices. This alignment contributes to a more meaningful and purpose-driven existence.

Contributing to a Meaningful Legacy: A clear vision often extends beyond personal ambitions to encompass a desire to positively impact the world. It empowers us to contribute to something greater than ourselves, leaving behind a lasting and meaningful legacy.

The journey towards clarity commenced with introspection and an honest assessment of my values, strengths, and aspirations. What truly mattered to me? What ignited my passion? Answering these questions unveiled the foundational elements of my vision.

Crafting the Vision: With newfound awareness, I began crafting a vivid vision for my life, envisioning the person I aimed to become, the experiences I desired, and the impact I sought to make. This vision became my guiding star, leading me out of darkness.

Clarity as a Compass: Embracing my vision, clarity became a powerful compass, directing me towards my true north. Decisions aligned with my vision, providing purpose and direction, illuminating the path through challenges and uncertainties.

Breaking the Shackles of Fear: With a clear vision, fear lost its grip, empowering me to take calculated risks and step outside my comfort zone. Each step forward was deliberate, moving me closer to the life I envisioned.

Fueling Motivation and Persistence: Clarity of vision renewed my motivation, inspiring me during moments of fatigue or setbacks. It fueled persistence, reminding me of the bigger picture, even in adversity.

Celebrating Progress, Embracing Evolution: Guided by my vision, I learned to celebrate progress and embrace the evolution of my goals. Clarity allowed for growth and adaptation, evolving with me as I discovered more about myself and the world.

The impact of clarity extended beyond my personal journey, inspiring and guiding others facing similar struggles. The light that guided me out of stagnation now had the potential to illuminate the paths of those around me.

Crafting a clear vision is vital for women restarting their lives after a break. It serves as a guiding light, offering direction and purpose amid transition and transformation. This vision is more than just goals; it shapes the path forward, providing clarity amidst chaos and fueling motivation and resilience.

A well-crafted vision acts as a roadmap for personal growth, encouraging women to redefine their identity, rediscover passions, and set new aspirations. It helps them embrace change, fostering a positive mindset and proactive approach to challenges. Vision becomes a source of strength during moments of doubt, driving persistence in the face of adversity.

Personal Mastery, fueled by a clear vision, sets the stage for skill development, learning, and self-discovery. It's about understanding and embracing unique strengths and talents, painting a picture of the ideal self. Crafting a vision is an ongoing process, requiring introspection, courage, and the willingness to dream big.

Aligning personal values with aspirations creates authenticity and fulfillment, guiding decisions and actions towards a life in harmony with one's core values. Amidst challenges, a well-defined vision provides the resilience needed to overcome obstacles, serving as motivation and inner strength.

Crafting a vision empowers women to navigate the complexities of restarting life with grace and determination. It's an indispensable tool for personal mastery, offering clarity, purpose, and resilience in the journey towards fulfillment and continuous growth.

Benefits of crafting a Vision

Crafting a vision involves considering various components

that collectively define the desired future state. These components serve as building blocks, providing clarity and direction for personal and professional growth. Here are key components of crafting a vision and how they are helpful:

- Clearly defining the purpose behind your vision gives it substance. It answers the question of "why" and provides a deep sense of meaning. When the purpose is clear, it becomes a driving force that keeps you motivated and focused on the long-term goal.
- Aligning your vision with your core values ensures authenticity. When your vision is in harmony with your values, it becomes a powerful motivator, guiding your decisions and actions. This alignment adds a sense of integrity to your journey.
- A specific and detailed vision offers a clear picture of the desired outcome. It helps in setting specific goals and milestones, making it easier to create actionable steps. Specificity enhances focus and provides a roadmap for the journey ahead.
- The language used in crafting the vision should be inspiring and motivational. It should evoke emotion and enthusiasm, creating a positive mindset. An inspiring vision language acts as a constant reminder of the possibilities and fuels the determination to achieve it.
- A vision is not about short-term gains; it's about the long-term impact. Considering a long-term perspective helps in sustaining motivation over time. It encourages perseverance during challenges by reminding you of the bigger picture.
- Life is dynamic, and circumstances change. A vision should allow for flexibility and adaptation. This

component is crucial for adjusting to unforeseen challenges, seizing new opportunities, and ensuring that the vision remains relevant and attainable.

- Creating a visual representation of the vision, such as a vision board, adds a tangible and creative dimension. It serves as a constant visual reminder, making the vision more vivid and compelling.

By carefully considering and integrating these components, individuals can craft a vision that not only serves as a roadmap but also as a source of inspiration and resilience in the pursuit of personal mastery and growth.

Clarity as a Compass

In the journey of restarting life after a break, clarity emerges as a guiding compass, illuminating the path forward. It is the North Star that provides direction, purpose, and a sense of orientation in times of uncertainty. As we navigate the complexities of rebuilding, clarity becomes an invaluable tool, shaping decisions, fostering resilience, and paving the way for a meaningful restart.

Components of Clarity

Self-reflection forms the basis of clarity, guiding individuals to delve into their values and beliefs, defining what truly matters. This introspection lays the groundwork for a vision aligned with personal principles, serving as a compass towards an authentic and fulfilling life.

Clarity in goal setting entails articulating specific, measurable, achievable, relevant, and time-bound (SMART) objectives. Clearly defined goals act as milestones, providing a roadmap and a sense of achievement as each step is reached.

Overwhelm Reduction: Clarity breaks down life complexities, simplifying overwhelming situations after a break. It helps focus on one step at a time, easing feelings of inundation.

Enhanced Decision-Making: Aligned choices with vision clarity sharpen decision-making. Clear vision aligns choices with the desired future, reflecting personal values and fostering purpose-driven decisions.

Resilience in Challenges: Clarity fosters a resilient mindset, transforming setbacks into stepping stones during life's restart. A clear vision provides strength and resilience, guiding individuals through adversity with purpose and determination.

How Clarity Facilitates Restarting Life

Identifying Priorities: Clarity helps individuals identify and prioritize essential elements in life, focusing energy and resources on what truly matters for well-being and success.

Building Confidence: Clarity establishes a foundation for self-trust by clarifying values, goals, and vision. This confidence is crucial for navigating challenges and making decisions after a break.

Creating a Roadmap for Growth: Clarity guides the crafting of a roadmap for personal mastery, setting goals for continuous growth, skill development, and self-improvement. A clear vision propels individuals towards becoming their best selves.

Defining the Journey Forward: Clarity serves as the compass steering individuals towards renewed purpose and fulfillment after restarting life. Its components, from self-reflection to goal setting, provide clear direction, reduce overwhelm, enhance decision-making, and instill resilience. As we embrace the journey forward, may clarity illuminate the path to a brighter and more empowered future.

Breaking the Shackles of Fear

In this section, we explore how clarity dismantles the shackles of fear, examining its components, understanding its importance, and uncovering its transformative role in the process of restarting life.

Components of Clarity in Breaking Fear's Shackles

Understanding Fears and Triggers: Clarity starts with self-awareness. Identifying fears and triggers empowers individuals to confront and overcome them by understanding their root causes.

Courageously Envisioning the Future: A bold and inspiring vision serves as a counterforce to fear. Defining a vision that deeply resonates motivates individuals to step out of their comfort zones and confront fears with courage and determination.

Importance of Clarity in Overcoming Fear

Informed Decision-Making: Clarity facilitates decision-making amidst fear by providing a clear vision to evaluate choices, ensuring alignment with overarching goals and reducing the paralyzing effects of fear.

Building Resilience: Clarity acts as a shield during life's uncertainties, fostering resilience. With a clear vision, individuals develop the strength to bounce back from setbacks, viewing fear as a temporary obstacle rather than an insurmountable barrier.

How Clarity of Vision Aids in Restarting Life After a Break

Overcoming Inertia with Motivation: Fear post-break can stall progress, but clarity provides motivation to move forward, breaking the cycle of stagnation.

Confidence Building: Clarity offers a roadmap, fostering confidence to navigate challenges, shifting from fear to conviction in restarting life.

Empowering Personal Growth: Self-awareness and vision work synergistically guiding personal growth, addressing fears and driving transformation.

Foundations for Conquering Fear: Decision-making

aligned with clarity and resilience are key in overcoming fear's barriers in the journey of restarting life.

Clarity in Fueling Motivation

Setting Clear Goals: Clarity starts with setting specific and achievable goals, providing direction and purpose. Clear goals naturally spark motivation as we know what we're working towards.

Aligning Vision with Personal Values: A vision is more powerful when it aligns with personal values, aspirations, and passions. The more relevant the vision, the stronger the motivation becomes, driving sustained success.

The Importance of Clarity in Fueling Motivation

Clarity is crucial for motivating us towards our goals, converting aspirations into actionable plans. Here's why clarity is essential for maintaining motivation:

Clear Goals Provide Direction: Well-defined goals give us a clear path to follow, boosting motivation to achieve them.

Alignment with Personal Values: When goals align with our values, motivation becomes intrinsic and resilient.

Tapping into Enthusiasm: A clear vision ignites passion, fueling us with energy and drive, even in the face of challenges.

Reducing Overwhelm: Clarity helps us focus on specific goals, preventing us from feeling overwhelmed and boosting motivation.

Resilience in Challenges: Clarity provides a long-term perspective, helping us view setbacks as temporary hurdles, maintaining motivation.

Empowering Decision-Making: Clear goals enhance decision-making, instilling confidence and purpose, sustaining motivation.

Adapting to Change: Clarity allows us to adapt goals and strategies, preventing demotivation when faced with unexpected challenges.

Fostering Self-Belief: Achieving clear goals builds confidence, renewing motivation to tackle bigger challenges.

Contributing to Satisfaction: Clarity deepens our connection to goals, leading to intrinsic satisfaction and continued effort.

Clarity fuels motivation by providing direction, tapping into intrinsic drivers, sustaining energy, and fostering resilience. It acts as a driving force, transforming aspirations into a motivational journey towards personal and professional fulfillment.

Clarity of vision isn't just a concept it's a powerful force driving motivation and persistence during life's restart. Components like clear goals, personal relevance, sustained energy, and resilience work together, propelling individuals forward. As one navigates life after a break, may clarity continue to fuel unwavering motivation and persistence.

In the profound process of restarting life after a break, celebrating progress and embracing evolution are essential practices that not only acknowledge the strides taken but also foster a mindset of continuous growth.

Steps to Achieve Clarity of Vision:

Reflect on personal and professional experiences, strengths, values, and passions to lay the foundation of self-awareness.

- Clearly articulate short-term and long-term career goals, identifying specific achievements, skills to develop, and preferred work environments.

Conduct research on industries and roles of interest, staying updated on market trends and potential challenges.

Connect with professionals in the desired field through

networking events, LinkedIn, and industry associations, seeking mentorship for valuable insights.

Evaluate current skills and invest time in acquiring or updating relevant skills through online courses or workshops.

Develop a step-by-step plan outlining actions required for reentering the workforce, including resume updates and attending networking events.

Consider internships, part-time work, or volunteer opportunities to gain practical experience and enhance marketability.

Stay open-minded to unexpected opportunities and be flexible in adapting the vision as needed, embracing learning from new experiences.

Consult with career counselors or coaches for professional guidance, setting realistic goals, and strategies for career reentry.

Acknowledge and celebrate milestones achieved along the way to boost morale and maintain motivation.

Having Clarity of Vision, I found the key to unlocking my potential and breaking free from the darkness that had held me captive. The journey from feeling stuck to finding my direction became a powerful, clear with a compelling vision. As the path ahead continues to unfold, I walk with purpose, guided by my vision that lights the way to a life of meaning and fulfillment.

3

Goal Setting

Every successful person begins with two beliefs: the future can be better than the present, and I have the power to make it so.

Embarking on a journey of Personal Mastery is an empowering endeavor, and at its core lies the strategic and intentional practice of goal setting. In this chapter, we delve into the profound significance of goal setting in the context of personal mastery, exploring its transformative role in restarting life after a break. As we unfold the pages, you'll discover the essential components of effective goal setting and the ways in which it can be your compass in the pursuit of a more fulfilling and purposeful life.

Personal Mastery is the continuous journey toward self-improvement and the realization of one's fullest potential. It involves cultivating a deep understanding of oneself, honing skills, and embracing a growth mindset. Goal setting serves as the linchpin in this process, providing the framework for intentional growth and development.

Goals in Personal Mastery are not mere checkpoints; they are expressions of purpose. Establishing meaningful goals aligns your efforts with your values and aspirations, giving each step a purposeful direction. As you restart life after a break, these purpose-driven goals become the building blocks of a more intentional and meaningful existence.

The Importance of Goal Setting

Clarity and Direction: Setting goals provides a clear vision amidst uncertainty. Like a compass, goals guide you toward a purposeful future, offering direction as you navigate life's challenges.

Motivation and Focus: Goals fuel determination and focus. They give you something to strive for, motivating you to push through obstacles and stay on track toward your objectives.

Measurable Progress: Goals enable you to track your achievements, making progress tangible. Celebrating small wins boosts confidence and reinforces your journey towards restarting life.

Time Management: Effective time management is encouraged through goal setting. Prioritizing tasks ensures that each moment contributes to your overarching goals, preventing procrastination.

Understanding Vision: Goal setting shapes our vision by providing clarity. Through introspection, we identify our values, passions, and long-term aspirations. By connecting goals to a defined vision, we give them purpose and significance.

Eliminating Uncertainty: Clear goal setting removes uncertainty. Vague goals like 'improve my career' lack precision for effective planning. Instead, specific objectives such as 'attain a managerial position within two years' provide a tangible target.

Enhancing Decision-Making: Clear goals act as decision-making guides. They offer direction when making choices, ensuring alignment with our vision. This streamlines efforts and ensures that decisions contribute to our desired outcome.

Goal setting fuels personal growth, pushing you out of your comfort zone and fostering learning. Each goal achieved propels you toward self-awareness and competence.

Amidst the challenges of restarting life after a break, goal setting offers a structured approach. It empowers intentional decision-making, helping you regain control and purpose.

Components of Effective Goal Setting

Effective goal setting involves several key components to ensure that your objectives are meaningful, achievable, and conducive to personal growth. Here are the essential components…

Clarity and Specificity: Clearly define your goal in specific terms. Vague goals make it challenging to create a focused plan of action.

Measurability: Establish concrete criteria to measure your progress. This allows you to track your achievements and adjust your approach if necessary.

Achievability: Ensure that your goals are realistic and attainable. Setting unattainable goals can lead to frustration and a sense of failure.

Time-Bound: Set a timeframe for achieving your goals, to add urgency and prevent procrastination.

Actionable Steps: Divide larger goals into smaller, manageable steps. This makes the process less overwhelming and allows for consistent progress.

Emotional Connection: Understand the deeper reasons behind each objective to boost motivation during challenging times.

Effective goal setting is not just about reaching the destination; it's about the journey and the continuous process of growth and self-discovery.

In the intricate art of goal setting, clarity and specificity stand as the cornerstones of success. Without a clear understanding of what you want to achieve and a specific plan to get there, goals can easily become elusive aspirations. This chapter explores the profound impact of clarity and specificity in goal setting and offers effective ways to cultivate these essential components.

The Need of Specificity in Goal Setting

Setting Measurable Milestones: Specificity involves breaking broad goals into measurable milestones. For instance, instead of aiming to "lose weight," specify a goal like "lose 10 pounds in three months." These measurable milestones create a clear roadmap for progress and allow for celebrating small victories.

Creating Actionable Steps: Specific goals are actionable, providing a clear roadmap with steps for success. Whether it's a career move or personal development, breaking goals into actionable steps makes the journey more manageable and less overwhelming.

Enhancing Focus and Commitment: Specific goals enhance focus and commitment by providing a precise target. This focus directs energy towards achieving the goal, increasing efficiency, and cultivating a sense of commitment crucial for overcoming obstacles and staying on course.

Effective Ways to Cultivate Clarity and Specificity

Visualization Techniques: Create a mental image of the desired outcome, immerse in the details, and feel the emotions associated with success. Visualization enhances our connection to the goal, making it more tangible and achievable.

Journaling and Reflection: Regular journaling and reflection provide a space for self-discovery and goal refinement. Write your aspirations, what success looks like to you, and the steps needed to get there. This helps refine goals over time.

S.M.A.R.T Goal Framework:

Adopt the SMART criteria: Specific, Measurable, Achievable, Relevant, and Time-bound. This framework provides a systematic approach to goal setting, ensuring that goals are clear, actionable, and aligned with your overall vision.

Seeking Feedback:

Seek input from mentors, peers, or friends for fresh perspectives on your goals. Their feedback can uncover blind spots and refine your aspirations. Clear and specific goals, with measurable milestones and effective cultivation, pave the way to success.

Measurability of Goal Setting

In goal setting, measurability plays a crucial role, transforming abstract aspirations into tangible achievements. Without a means of measuring progress, goals risk becoming elusive ideals rather than actionable targets. This section explores the significance of measurability in goal setting and outlines effective strategies for ensuring that your objectives remain within quantifiable reach.

The Importance of Measuring Progress

Creating Accountability: One of the primary functions of measurability is to create a sense of accountability. When you can track progress through measurable milestones, you instill a sense of responsibility for your own success. It becomes clear whether you're on track, falling behind, or exceeding expectations.

Boosting Motivation: Measurable goals provide a constant source of motivation. Small wins along the way, measured and acknowledged, fuel your enthusiasm and commitment. Regularly witnessing progress, no matter how incremental, reinforces the belief that your efforts are leading to meaningful outcomes.

Adapting Strategies: Measurability allows for dynamic strategy adjustments. If you notice that you're not progressing as expected, the ability to measure your advancement enables you to identify areas for improvement and adjust your approach. This adaptability is essential for overcoming challenges and staying on course.

Cultivating a Measurable Mindset

Regular Check-Ins: Schedule check-ins to reflect, celebrate achievements, and adjust strategies. Consistent evaluation keeps you connected to your goals and underscores the importance of measurability

Feedback and Evaluation: Get feedback from mentors, friends, or peers to see how you're doing. Their advice helps you make your goals better.

Celebrate Achievements: Celebrate when you reach your goals, big or small. It helps you keep going and feel good about your progress.

In goal setting, measuring your progress helps you stay accountable, motivated, and able to change course if needed. Using clear metrics and tracking tools makes your goals more achievable and gives you confidence along the way.

Setting ambitious goals is admirable, but without a foundation of achievability, aspirations may remain just dreams. This section explores the crucial concept of achievability in goal setting, emphasizing the need for realistic objectives and offering practical strategies to transform your goals from lofty ideals into attainable milestones.

The Significance of Achievability

Mitigating Overwhelm: Break down big goals into smaller, achievable steps to avoid feeling overwhelmed. This makes progress steady and manageable.

Sustaining Motivation: Setting goals that are within reach keeps you motivated. Consistent progress, no matter how small, shows that success is possible and keeps you going.

Building Confidence: Achieving realistic goals boosts your confidence. Each success builds on the last, making you more confident, especially when things get tough.

Strategies for Achieving Realistic Goals

Assess Your Current Reality: Before setting a goal, understand your starting point, resources, and constraints. This realistic assessment informs the feasibility of your objectives and helps you set achievable targets based on your unique circumstances.

Break Down into Smaller Steps: Divide larger goals into smaller, manageable steps. Instead of aiming for an overwhelming outcome, focus on the immediate actions that will propel you forward. This approach not only makes the journey less daunting but also allows for consistent progress.

Set Incremental Targets: Gradual progression enables you to adjust and learn along the way. Celebrate each small achievement as it contributes to the overall success of your pursuit.

Consider External Factors: Consider your environment, available resources, and potential obstacles. Adjust your goals to align with these factors, ensuring that they remain within reach.

Cultivating an Achievable Mindset

Regular Review and Adjustment: Circumstances may change, and a goal that was initially achievable may need modification. Regular check-ins allow for flexibility and ensure that your objectives remain relevant and attainable.

Seek Support and Guidance: Share your goals with mentors, friends, or family who can provide valuable insights. External perspectives can offer a realistic assessment of achievability and provide constructive feedback.

Celebrate Small Wins: Recognizing and appreciating your progress, no matter how modest, reinforces a positive mindset. Small celebrations contribute to a sense of accomplishment and motivate continued effort.

Setting achievable goals bridges the gap between dreams and reality. Break goals into smaller steps, set targets, and consider outside factors to stay on track. This mindset turns your journey into one of progress, motivation, and reaching your dreams.

Time-Bound Goal Setting: The Essence of Productivity and Achievement

Time is an invaluable resource, and in the realm of goal setting, it becomes a strategic dimension that shapes our endeavors. This section explores the significance of time-bound goal setting, shedding light on the benefits it offers and providing practical insights on how to infuse your objectives with a sense of urgency.

The Benefits of Time-Bound Goals

Enhanced Focus and Priority: Setting deadlines improves focus and prioritization. Knowing you have limited time helps you use it wisely and concentrate on tasks that move you closer to your goal.

Preventing Procrastination: Deadlines prevent

procrastination by making you accountable. They push you to act promptly instead of delaying tasks, keeping momentum and progress going.

Measurable Progress and Evaluation: Time-bound goals make progress measurable. With clear deadlines, you can track your advancement regularly, making it easier to adjust your strategies based on timely feedback.

Strategies for Achieving Time-Bound Goals

Set Clear Deadlines: Whether short-term or long-term, a defined timeframe adds structure to your objectives. Consider breaking down larger goals into smaller tasks with corresponding deadlines to ensure a steady pace of progress.

Prioritize and Sequencing: Prioritize your goals, determine which goals are most time sensitive and arrange your efforts accordingly. This approach prevents feeling overwhelmed and allows you to focus on one goal at a time.

Utilize Time Management Tools: Leverage time management tools and techniques to enhance your efficiency. Calendars, planners, and productivity apps can help you allocate time effectively, set reminders for deadlines, and create a visual representation of your time bound goals.

Regular Review and Adjustment: Regularly review your time-bound goals to ensure they're realistic and adaptable. Life changes, so adjust your timelines accordingly, considering external factors and your shifting priorities.

Steps to Cultivating a Time Conscious Mindset

Develop a Schedule: Create a daily or weekly schedule that incorporates specific time slots for working toward your goals. By integrating goal related tasks into your routine, you ensure consistent progress and foster a habit of time consciousness.

Practice Time Blocking: Time blocking involves dedicating specific blocks of time to particular tasks. Allocate focused time periods for working on your goals. This practice minimizes distractions and optimizes productivity, ensuring that you make the most of the time available.

Reward Time Management: Incorporate a reward system tied to effective time management. Celebrate meeting deadlines and achieving goals within the specified timeframe. Positive reinforcement creates a connection between time-bound accomplishments and the gratification of success.

Time-bound objectives act as the tempo, guiding and driving progress forward. Set clear deadlines, prioritize effectively, and use time management tools to give your goals the energy they need. A mindful approach to time becomes the conductor, directing the pace of achievement on your path to success.

Actionable Steps in Goal Setting: Transforming Intentions into Results

Setting goals is a powerful exercise, but the true magic happens when those goals are translated into actionable steps. This section explores the transformative nature of actionable steps in goal setting, shedding light on their importance and providing practical guidance on how to turn aspirations into concrete achievements.

The Significance of Actionable Steps

Bridging the Gap Between Vision and Reality: Actionable steps serve as the bridge between your vision and the tangible reality of achievement. While goals provide the destination, actionable steps chart the course, guiding your efforts and ensuring a purposeful journey.

Overcoming Inertia and Procrastination: The nature of actionable steps is inherently dynamic, serving as antidotes to inertia and procrastination. They break down larger goals into manageable tasks, making progress more approachable and reducing the likelihood of feeling overwhelmed.

Fostering Consistency and Momentum: Consistency is the bedrock of success, and actionable steps foster a consistent approach to goal pursuit. By integrating specific tasks into your routine, you create a rhythm that sustains momentum, propelling you closer to your objectives with each deliberate action.

Strategies for Defining Actionable Steps

Break Down Goals into Smaller Tasks: Start by breaking big goals into smaller, manageable tasks. This makes them easier to tackle and helps you make progress step by step.

Prioritize and Sequence: Once you have your tasks, prioritize them based on what's most important and put them in order. This helps you focus on what matters most and makes your efforts more efficient.

Assign Deadlines to Each Task: Give each task a deadline to create a sense of urgency. This keeps you on track and provides a clear timeline for your progress.

Cultivating an Action-Oriented Mindset

Create a Daily Action Plan: Outline the specific tasks you aim to accomplish each day, aligning them with your overarching goals. This plan becomes a tangible roadmap for your daily efforts, keeping you focused and on track.

Visualize the Execution: Visualization is a powerful tool. Picture yourself successfully completing each actionable step. This enhances your belief in the feasibility of your tasks and creates a positive mindset for execution.

Celebrate Milestones along the Way: As you complete each actionable step, take a moment to celebrate the achievement. Acknowledging these milestones reinforces a positive feedback loop, motivating you to tackle subsequent tasks with renewed energy and determination.

Course Correct and Adapt: Stay flexible in your journey of taking action. Evaluate progress regularly, listen to feedback, and adjust your approach as needed. This keeps you responsive to changes and challenges.

Actionable steps drive progress and success. Break goals into manageable tasks, prioritize well, and stay focused on taking consistent action. This turns intentions into real results, showcasing the power of deliberate steps towards achievement.

The Heart of Goal Setting: Establishing Emotional Connections

In goal setting, our emotional connection to our aspirations is crucial for success. This section explores why having this connection matters, outlines its benefits, and provides advice on how to nurture it during the pursuit of our goals.

The Importance of Emotional Connection

Intrinsic Motivation: Emotional ties to our goals fuel intrinsic motivation. When goals align with our values, passions, or personal growth, our drive to pursue them comes from within and remains strong even when faced with challenges.

Sustainability and Resilience: Goals that have emotional significance are more likely to last. When obstacles arise, the emotional connection acts as a source of resilience, helping individuals bounce back, learn, and keep moving forward.

Meaning and Fulfillment: Emotional connections add depth and fulfillment to goal achievement. Goals that resonate emotionally aren't just tasks to complete but contribute to a sense of purpose and satisfaction. This emotional fulfillment is a lasting reward beyond mere accomplishment.

Benefits of Emotional Connection with Goals

Enhanced Commitment: Emotional ties increase commitment to goals. When individuals deeply care about what they're working toward, they're more likely to stick with it through challenges and setbacks.

Heightened Focus and Concentration: Goals with emotional meaning draw sharper focus and concentration. The emotional connection directs attention to tasks that matter most for achieving meaningful goals.

Increased Resilience to Setbacks: Emotional connections to goals build resilience in tough times. People see obstacles as temporary hurdles rather than roadblocks because of their emotional attachment, motivating them to keep going despite adversity.

Strategies for Cultivating Emotional Connection

Reflect on Personal Values and Passions: Take time to think about what matters most to you and what you're passionate about. Consider how your goals align with these inner aspects of yourself. The closer your goals match your core values, the stronger your emotional connection will be.

Visualize Success with Emotion: Picture yourself achieving your goals and pay attention to how it makes you feel. Visualization helps strengthen the emotional bond between you and your goals. It connects your aspirations with your feelings of success.

Connect Goals to Larger Purpose: Link your goals to a bigger purpose or mission in your life. Understand how achieving these goals fits into your overall vision. This connection makes your goals more meaningful and gives them a deeper sense of purpose.

Regularly Revisit and Reinforce Connections: Check in with your goals regularly and see if they still resonate with you emotionally. As you grow and change, your values and passions may shift. Reflecting on your goals ensures they stay aligned with how you feel, keeping your emotional connection strong and relevant.

The emotional connection between our aspirations and who we are at our core turns goal pursuit into a satisfying journey. By nurturing emotional resonance, goals become more than just destinations; they become meaningful milestones in a larger story of personal growth and fulfillment

Benefits of Goal Setting for Women on Sabbatical

Clarity of Purpose: Goal setting helps you figure out what you want professionally and personally after your break. It's like a roadmap for your future, whether you're going back to your old job or exploring new opportunities.

Skill Development and Improvement: You can use goal setting to learn new skills or brush up on old ones during your break. This keeps you competitive in the job market and ready for whatever your career throws at you when you return.

Boosting Confidence: Setting and reaching goals, even small ones, can make you feel more confident. This is crucial when you're getting back into the workforce, helping you feel sure of yourself in interviews, networking, and new job situations.

Networking and Professional Presence: Goals related to networking and building a professional image can help you connect with people in your field. This is key to finding job opportunities and staying up-to-date with what's happening in your industry.

Work-Life Balance: Goal setting lets you set boundaries and find the right balance between work and life. This makes it easier to transition back to work without sacrificing your personal well-being.

Steps to Achieve Success in goal setting:

Self-Reflection: Reflect on your strengths, passions, and the skills you want to leverage in your next role. Define your values and what work-life balance means to you.

Define Career Goals: Clearly articulate your career goals. Consider the type of role, industry, and work environment that aligns with your aspirations. Break down long-term goals into smaller, achievable steps.

Skill Development: Identify skills in demand within your industry and acquire or enhance them during your sabbatical. This could involve online courses, workshops, certifications, or practical projects.

Networking Goals: Set specific networking goals, such as attending industry events, joining professional groups, or connecting with former colleagues. Leverage online platforms like LinkedIn to build and maintain your professional network.

Resume Update Your Online Presence: Make sure your resume and LinkedIn profile are up-to-date. Show off your skills and accomplishments so potential employers can see what you bring to the table.

Develop a Job Search Strategy: Figure out which companies you want to work for and use online job platforms to find openings. Reach out to your network for job leads and advice.

Prepare for Interviews: Practice answering common interview questions, especially ones about your time off. Show how your sabbatical experiences make you a better candidate.

Evaluate Offers and Negotiate: When you get job offers, think carefully about whether they fit with your goals and values. Don't be afraid to negotiate to make sure you get what you want.

Create a Transition Plan: Plan how you'll transition back into work, including things like childcare and flexible work arrangements. This helps make the return smoother.

Goal setting is a powerful tool for women returning to work after a break. It gives them direction and helps them make a plan to achieve their professional goals. By setting clear, achievable goals, women on sabbatical can find purpose and overcome challenges with determination. Goal setting isn't just about getting back to work; it's about personal growth and realizing your potential. Through intentional goalsetting, women on a break can redefine their career paths and become the best versions of themselves.

Identifying Mindset

"Instead of worrying about what you cannot control shift your energy to what you can create." **- Roy T. Bennett**

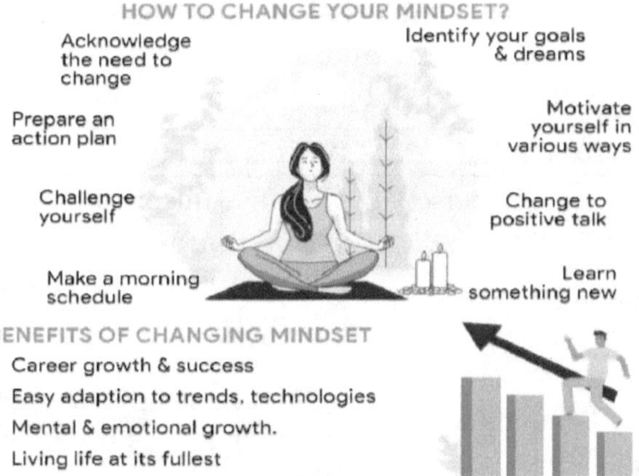

A person's mindset is crucial for tackling tasks effectively, whether it's reaching professional goals, studying for exams, or learning new skills.

Achieving personal mastery goes beyond skill development and goal-setting; it requires understanding your mindset—the lens through which you see the world.

In this chapter, we explore the importance of mindset in personal mastery, its components, and how it guides those restarting their lives after a break.

Mindset, our mental outlook, greatly influences personal mastery. A growth mindset sees challenges as opportunities, while a fixed mindset views them as obstacles. Cultivating a growth mindset is key for mastering both personal and professional life, particularly after a break.

To identify your mindset, it's important to understand the differences between them.

Individuals with fixed mindsets believe their abilities are fixed and rely heavily on their existing intelligence and talent. Conversely, those with growth mindsets are open to learning and believe they can develop their skills with effort.

The comparison table below illustrates differences in thinking between fixed and growth mindsets, aiding in identifying your mindset based on these examples.

What is a fixed mindset?	What is a growth mindset?
Feedback is a personal attack against me.	There's value in the feedback I get.
I'm either good at it or I'm not.	I can learn to do it and in time, I may become good at it with practice.
I am who I am. It's too late to change now.	I'm constantly learning and changing to be a better version of myself.
I already know everything I need to.	Learning is lifelong, there's still so much that I can learn.
Why try if I'm going to fail?	Failures are learning opportunities and can prepare me to do better next time.
This is out of my league.	This looks challenging. Let me try to work on it and see how it goes.

Changing from a Fixed Mindset to a Growth Mindset: If you find yourself with a fixed mindset, don't fret. The good news is, you can change it with effort. The brain's neuroplasticity shows that you can train it to have a growth mindset. Here's how.

Identify Your Fixed Mindset Voice: Explore to identify negative self-talk, using example statements to recognize a fixed mindset. If you believe talent is fixed and can't be improved, you may limit yourself from trying new things.

Acknowledge Your Choice: Mindset affects how we face challenges. Choose to see failures as learning opportunities rather than dead ends. Opt for a growth mindset to expand your abilities and intelligence.

Replace Fixed Mindset Statements: Swap self-limiting thoughts with growth mindset alternatives. Use positive affirmations and focus on the journey of learning. Embrace challenges and use the word "yet" to remind yourself of potential growth

Ask yourself growth mindset questions such as:

What can I learn from this experience?

What value can I take away from this feedback?

How do I intend to follow through on my plan?

Taking action: A growth mindset is about being optimistic. It involves putting in the hard work that is needed to achieve your goals. Once you have a clear plan of action in place, Taking the required steps and execute it to achieve what you desire.

Components of a Growth Mindset

Openness to Learning: A growth mindset thrives on a genuine desire to learn and adapt. Embracing new experiences and seeking knowledge fosters personal growth and resilience.

Resilience in the Face of Challenges: Individuals with a growth mindset view setbacks as temporary and valuable learning experiences. Resilience becomes a key component in navigating life's uncertainties.

Positive Self-Talk: The narrative we create about ourselves significantly influences our actions. Cultivating a growth mindset involves replacing self-limiting beliefs with positive affirmations and constructive self-talk.

Life often brings unexpected interruptions, such as personal reasons, career changes, or unforeseen circumstances. During these times, mindset becomes crucial for bouncing back. A growth mindset sees breaks as chances for self-reflection, learning, and adaptability, smoothing the transition to the next phase of life.

Mindsets aren't fixed; they can be improved and adjusted. Identify your mindset and consider changing it if necessary. A shift in mindset can improve your life, and there are tools to help you. Embrace growth and harness the power of mindset for personal mastery. Cultivating a growth mindset helps navigate challenges with resilience and seize opportunities to restart and redefine your path after a break.

How will Identifying Mindset help Women on Sabbatical get back to Work

Identifying mindset is key for women returning to work after a sabbatical. It helps them navigate the transition effectively and empowers them in the professional realm. Let's see how recognizing and cultivating the right mindset can help these women get back to work.

Building Confidence: Acknowledging the mindset is the first step. Women on sabbatical may have experienced a shift in confidence during their time away from the workforce. Identifying this change is vital for targeted improvement. Cultivating a growth mindset involves recognizing that confidence is not fixed but can be developed over time. Embracing new challenges, setting small achievable goals, and celebrating successes contribute to rebuilding and boosting confidence.

Overcoming Self-Doubt: Recognizing negative thought patterns and limiting beliefs is essential in overcoming these mental barriers. Transforming self-doubt requires a conscious effort to challenge and reframe negative thoughts. Embracing a growth mindset involves viewing setbacks as opportunities to learn and grow, gradually replacing self-doubt with self-empowerment.

Adapting to Change: Returning to work often involves adapting to changes in technology, industry trends, and workplace dynamics. Recognizing the need for adaptability is crucial for a successful transition. Cultivating a growth mindset involves embracing change as a natural part of the learning process. Women on sabbatical can update their skills, seek training opportunities, and stay informed about industry advancements to navigate the evolving work landscape.

Networking and Relationship Building: A mindset shift may be required to approach networking with confidence, especially after a break. Recognizing the importance of connections is crucial for professional growth. Adopting a growth mindset involves viewing networking as a collaborative process rather than a transaction. Women can actively seek mentorship, attend industry events, and participate in networking groups to build meaningful professional relationships.

Balancing Work and Life: Recognizing the importance of work-life balance is essential for women returning after a sabbatical. Identifying potential challenges in managing responsibilities is crucial. Cultivating a growth mindset involves approaching work-life balance as an ongoing process of adjustment. Women can set realistic expectations, communicate openly with employers about their needs, and prioritize self-care to achieve a harmonious balance.

Embracing Lifelong Learning: Acknowledging the need

for continuous learning is essential in a rapidly evolving professional landscape. A growth mindset involves adopting a proactive approach to learning. Women returning from a sabbatical can enroll in courses, attend workshops, and stay informed about industry trends to enhance their skills and knowledge.

Identifying mindset is essential for women returning to work after a sabbatical. By embracing a growth mindset, they can tackle challenges, boost confidence, and seize opportunities for personal and professional growth. Returning to work isn't just about coming back; it's a path toward new possibilities and development.

5

Communication Skills

"Good communication is the Bridge between confusion and clarity." **– Nat Turner**

Effective communication involves both active listening and clear expression. It's not just one skill but a combination of verbal and nonverbal cues, along with attentive listening. Communication is crucial for personal mastery, impacting every aspect of life. This chapter delves into the importance of communication skills, their components, and how improving them can lead to transformative growth.

The Importance of Communication Skills in Personal Mastery

Building Relationships: Communication is the bridge that connects individuals. Effective communication skills foster the development of meaningful relationships, both personally and professionally.

Personal Mastery involves understanding the nuances of communication, including verbal and non-verbal cues, to build trust and rapport with others.

Conflict Resolution: A crucial aspect of Personal Mastery is the ability to navigate conflicts with grace and empathy. Effective communication skills are essential in resolving disputes, finding common ground, and maintaining harmonious relationships.

Through clear and assertive communication, individuals can address conflicts constructively, fostering an environment of understanding and collaboration.

Self-Expression: Personal Mastery requires self-awareness and the ability to express thoughts and feelings authentically. Communication skills empower individuals to articulate their ideas, emotions, and aspirations effectively.

Expressing oneself with clarity and confidence contributes to a sense of personal empowerment and fosters a deeper connection with others.

Components of Effective Communication Skills

Active Listening: Effective communication starts with active listening. It involves understanding others' perspectives and responding thoughtfully, fostering empathy, strengthening relationships, and promoting collaboration.

Clear and Concise Expression: Personal mastery requires clear communication. Articulating thoughts clearly ensures accurate understanding, while avoiding ambiguity and jargon facilitates effective communication across contexts.

Non-Verbal Communication: Non-verbal cues like body language are crucial in communication. Being aware of these cues enhances communication effectiveness and fosters authentic connections.

The Role of Communication Skills in Personal Development

Self-Reflection: Effective communication requires self-reflection. Personal Mastery involves assessing and refining communication skills. Introspection helps identify areas for improvement and enhances connection with others.

Adaptability: Personal Mastery means adjusting communication styles to various contexts. Flexibility in communication helps navigate diverse situations and build rapport. Being adaptable fosters collaboration and contributes to growth.

How to Improve Your Communication Skills

Practice Active Listening: Effective communicators engage by giving affirmative replies and asking follow-up questions, showing they're attentive and listening.

Focus on Nonverbal Communication: Mastering nonverbal cues prevents miscommunication and signals interest. Pay attention to facial expressions and body language, as they affect first impressions.

Manage Emotions: Managing emotions is crucial for clear communication and personal well-being. Avoid letting strong emotions interfere in professional settings to prevent conflict.

Seek Feedback: Ask for honest feedback from friends and colleagues to understand how you're perceived. Being open to other viewpoints helps improve communication and relationships.

Practice Public Speaking: Seek public speaking opportunities to develop communication and presentation skills. Regular practice in front of groups helps identify strengths and weaknesses.

Develop a Filter: Effective communicators modulate their expressions based on social context. Developing a filter ensures appropriate communication and maintains decorum to avoid conflicts.

Practical Strategies for Enhancing Communication Skills

Communication Workshops and Training: Participate in workshops and training programs focused on communication skills. Learn about effective verbal and non-verbal communication, active listening, and clear expression.

Seeking Feedback: Actively seek feedback from peers, mentors, or colleagues. Constructive feedback helps identify strengths and areas for improvement, contributing to personal growth.

Journaling: Keep a communication journal to reflect on daily interactions, identify patterns, and set improvement goals. Journaling enhances self-awareness and tracks progress in communication skills.

Role-Playing: Engage in role-playing scenarios to practice communication skills, especially for challenging situations like negotiations or public speaking.

Remember, mastering communication skills is a lifelong journey. Consistent practice, a genuine desire for improvement, and commitment to self-reflection contribute to continuous growth in personal and professional development.

Effective communication is essential for women on sabbatical returning to the workforce. Developing communication skills can help convey strengths, navigate professional relationships, and adapt to workplace dynamics. Here are strategies to achieve this:

Confident Self-Presentation: Present oneself confidently during interviews and interactions. Practice articulating experiences and seek feedback on presentation skills.

Networking and Relationship Building: Foster collaboration and networking with colleagues and employers. Attend events, join networking groups, and practice active listening.

Resume and Cover Letter Crafting: Showcase qualifications effectively through clear communication. Tailor documents, highlight relevant skills, and seek feedback.

Effective Interviewing Skills: Excel in interviews with strong verbal and non-verbal communication. Practice common questions, participate in mock interviews, and focus on body language.

Negotiation and Assertiveness: Negotiate job offers assertively with clear communication. Understand value, practice assertive communication, and seek professional coaching if needed.

Adapting to Workplace Culture: Navigate office dynamics through effective communication. Observe, seek guidance, and engage in open communication to understand and adapt to workplace culture.

Continuous Learning and Industry Updates: Stay informed about industry trends to enhance professional communication. Commit to ongoing learning through workshops, webinars, and networking.

Balancing Personal and Professional Communication: Maintain a balance between personal and professional communication. Set boundaries, communicate expectations, and prioritize effective communication.

Leveraging Digital Communication Tools: Utilize digital tools for effective communication in the modern workplace. Familiarize with tools and practice professional communication through email and virtual meetings.

Emotional Intelligence: Develop emotional intelligence for positive relationships and effective communication.

Practice self-awareness, empathy, and develop strategies to navigate challenging situations effectively.

Developing communication skills is a strategic investment for women on sabbatical aiming to reenter the workforce. By focusing on these skills, they can enhance their confidence, build meaningful relationships, and navigate the complexities of the professional environment successfully. Continuous practice, feedback-seeking, and a commitment to growth will contribute to their effectiveness in communication and overall success in their career comeback.

6

Focus

"When you focus on the small steps, bigger steps automatically happen."
-Victoria J Brown

In the pursuit of Personal Mastery, one of the key pillars that stands tall is the ability to maintain focus. This chapter delves into the significance of having focus, exploring why it is crucial for personal development, the components that contribute to a focused mindset, and practical strategies to cultivate and sustain it.

The Importance of Focus in Personal Mastery

Precision of Purpose: Having focus provides clarity of purpose. It allows individuals to define their goals with precision, enabling a more targeted and effective approach to personal development. Personal Mastery begins with a clear understanding of one's objectives, and focus acts as the compass guiding the way.

Efficiency and Productivity: Focus is the linchpin of efficiency and productivity. With a concentrated mind, tasks are approached with intent, minimizing distractions and optimizing the use of time and energy. Personal Mastery involves honing the ability to achieve goals with maximum effectiveness, making focus an invaluable asset.

Flexibility in the Face of Challenges: The journey of personal mastery is not without challenges. Having focus cultivates resilience by allowing individuals to stay committed to their objectives despite obstacles. A focused mindset empowers individuals to navigate setbacks and maintain progress on their path of personal development.

Components of a Focused Mindset

Precision in Goals: Defining clear, specific, and achievable goals is a fundamental component of focus. Breaking down larger goals into smaller, actionable steps enhances focus by providing manageable milestones.

Mindfulness and Presence: Mindfulness practices contribute significantly to focus. Being present in the current moment allows individuals to direct their attention to the task at hand, reducing the impact of external distractions. Techniques such as meditation and deep breathing foster a focused and centered mindset.

Prioritization and Time Management: Focus involves effective prioritization and time management. Identifying and tackling high-priority tasks ensures that energy is directed toward activities that align with personal development goals.

The Role of Focus in Decision-Making

Informed Decision-Making: A focused mind can weigh

options more objectively, considering the potential impact on personal development goals.

Personal mastery involves making intentional choices that align with one's values, and focus is the compass that guides these decisions.

Reducing Decision Fatigue: An unfocused mind can be overwhelmed by decision fatigue, leading to poor choices and a lack of progress. Maintaining focus streamlines decision-making, reducing mental fatigue associated with an abundance of choices.

Personal mastery requires consistency in decision-making, and focus serves as a tool to streamline this process.

Strategies for Cultivating and Sustaining Focus

Mindfulness Practices: Incorporate mindfulness practices into your routine, such as meditation or mindfulness exercises. These practices enhance your ability to stay present and focused on the midst of distractions.

Goal Setting and Planning: Set clear, measurable goals and create a detailed plan to achieve them. Break down larger goals into smaller, manageable tasks, allowing for a more focused and systematic approach to personal development.

Eliminating Distractions: Identify and minimize external distractions. Create a conducive environment for focus by decluttering your workspace, turning off unnecessary notifications, and setting dedicated periods of uninterrupted work or reflection.

Time Allocation: Implement time allocating techniques to block specific periods for focused work or personal development activities. This strategy helps protect your time from being consumed by less important tasks.

Regular Reflection: Engage in regular reflection to assess your progress, challenges, and areas for improvement.

Adjust your goals and strategies based on these reflections to stay on the path of personal mastery.

Mastering the art of focus in life is a transformative skill that can enhance productivity, effectiveness, and overall well-being.

Here are practical strategies to help you cultivate and sustain focus in various aspects of your life:

Define Clear Goals: Establish clear and specific goals for different areas of your life, such as career, relationships, health, and personal development. Clarity in your objectives provides a roadmap for where to direct your focus.

Prioritize Tasks: Identify and prioritize tasks based on their importance and urgency. Focusing on high-priority tasks first ensures that you are allocating your energy to activities that align with your overall goals.

Break Down Complex Tasks: Divide larger tasks into smaller, more manageable components. Tackling one step at a time helps prevent overwhelm and allows you to maintain focus on each individual aspect of the task.

Practice Mindfulness: Engage in mindfulness practices, such as meditation and deep breathing exercises. These activities train your mind to stay present, reducing the impact of external distractions and enhancing your ability to focus.

Limit Multitasking: While multitasking may seem efficient, it often leads to decreased overall focus and quality of work. Instead, focus on one task at a time to ensure that your attention is fully dedicated to each activity.

Create a Dedicated Workspace: Establish a dedicated and organized workspace. Minimize distractions, and ensure that your environment is conducive to focused work or reflection. A clutter-free and purposeful workspace can significantly enhance your ability to concentrate.

Set Realistic Time Limits: Allocate specific time limits for tasks. Setting realistic deadlines creates a sense of urgency, preventing procrastination, and helping you maintain focus within a defined timeframe.

Take Breaks Strategically: Incorporate short breaks between focused work sessions. Breaks help refresh your mind and prevent burnout, allowing you to return to tasks with renewed focus and energy.

Eliminate Unnecessary Distractions: Identify and eliminate or minimize distractions in your environment. Turn off non-essential notifications, silence your phone, and communicate boundaries to those around you to create a focused work environment.

Practice Digital Detox: Designate specific periods during the day for a digital detox. Disconnecting from technology, especially social media, allows you to reclaim your attention and focus on meaningful activities.

Use Focus Techniques: Experiment with focus techniques, such as the Pomodoro Technique or time blocking. These methods help structure your time, allowing you to work in focused intervals and take breaks deliberately.

Cultivate Mindful Listening: Practice mindful listening in conversations. Give your full attention to the speaker, avoid interrupting, and engage in active listening. This not only enhances your understanding but also strengthens your interpersonal relationships.

Set Boundaries: Establish clear boundaries between work and personal life. Define specific times for work, relaxation, and social activities to prevent one aspect from encroaching on another, allowing you to focus on the task at hand.

Stay Physically Active: Regular physical activity has been linked to improved focus and cognitive function.

Incorporate exercise into your routine to enhance your overall well-being and sharpen your ability to concentrate.

Reflect and Adjust: Regularly reflect on your focus habits and effectiveness. Assess what strategies are working for you and make adjustments as needed. Personalize your approach to align with your unique preferences and challenges.

Mastering the art of focus is an ongoing journey that involves self-awareness, discipline, and continuous refinement of your habits. By incorporating these strategies into your daily life, you can cultivate a focused mindset that empowers you to navigate the complexities of life with intention and clarity.

How will having focus help women on sabbatical get back to work

Having focus is a crucial asset for women on sabbatical seeking to reenter the workforce. The ability to concentrate on specific goals, tasks, and the overall transition process plays a significant role in their successful return. Here's how having focus can benefit women on sabbatical and contribute to a smoother transition back to work:

Clarity of Career Goals: Focus provides clarity of career goals, helping women on sabbatical define what they want to achieve upon reentering the workforce. This clarity enables a targeted job search, making it more likely to find positions that align with their aspirations and skills.

Efficient Skill Development: Focus allows for efficient skill development during the sabbatical period. Women on sabbatical can use focused periods to upskill or reskill, ensuring they are equipped with the latest knowledge and competencies relevant to their chosen field.

Strategic Networking: Focused networking efforts can help women on sabbatical build meaningful connections.

Networking with professionals in their industry during the sabbatical can open doors to potential job opportunities, mentorship, and valuable insights into the current job market.

Tailored Job Search: Focused job search strategies allow for a more tailored approach. Women on sabbatical can concentrate their efforts on positions that align with their skills, experiences, and career goals, increasing the likelihood of finding a suitable role.

Effective Resume and Cover Letter Crafting: Focus contributes to the effective crafting of resumes and cover letters. Women on sabbatical can highlight their achievements, skills gained during the break, and how their experiences align with the requirements of potential employers.

Confident Interview Performance: A focused mindset contributes to confident interview performance. Women on sabbatical can articulate their experiences, address potential gaps in their work history, and convey their readiness to contribute effectively to a new workplace.

Adaptability to Workplace Changes: Focus aids in adapting to changes within the workplace. As industries evolve, women on sabbatical with a focused mindset can quickly adapt to new technologies, work methodologies, and organizational cultures, positioning themselves as valuable assets to employers.

Effective Time Management: Focus enhances time management skills. Efficiently managing time allows women on sabbatical to balance job search activities with personal responsibilities, making the transition back to work more seamless.

Resilience in the Face of Challenges: A focused mindset cultivates resilience. Women on sabbatical may face challenges during the job search or upon returning to work. With focus, they can navigate setbacks, learn from experiences, and persevere with determination.

Balancing Professional and Personal Priorities: Focus helps in balancing professional and personal priorities. Women on sabbatical can effectively manage their time, set boundaries, and allocate focus to both work-related and personal development activities, fostering a balanced and sustainable approach.

Focus is a cornerstone of personal mastery, guiding individuals toward their goals with intention and clarity. By understanding the importance of focus, recognizing its components, and implementing practical strategies to cultivate and sustain it, individuals can enhance their journey of personal development and achieve a greater sense of mastery over their lives.

Having focus is a valuable asset for women on sabbatical, contributing to their overall preparedness, confidence, and resilience as they transition back to work. Whether it's in skill development, networking, job search, or adapting to workplace changes, a focused mindset empowers women to navigate the challenges of reentering the workforce with purpose and clarity.

7

Building Habits

"Depending on what they are, our habits will either make us or break us. We become what we repeatedly do."

– Sean covey

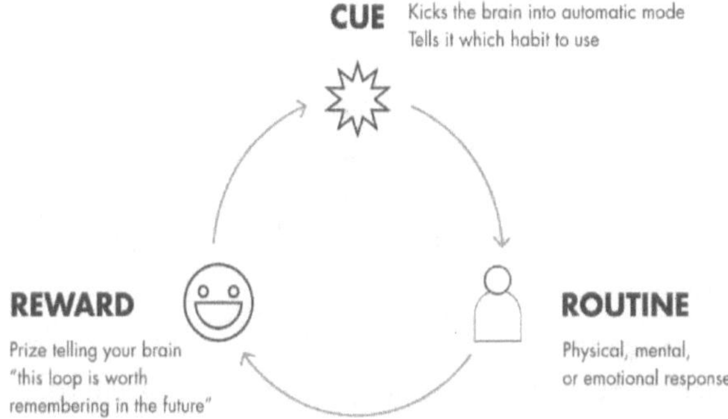

Habits are the invisible architects of our lives, shaping our daily routines, behaviors, and ultimately, our destiny. In the pursuit of personal mastery, the cultivation of intentional habits plays a pivotal role. This chapter explores the importance of building habits, delving into the components that contribute to habit formation and offering insights into how habits can propel individuals on the path of personal mastery.

Habits are a path to changing your identity. The most practical way to change who you are is to change what you do. Your habits shape your identity and your identity shapes your habits it is a two-way street. The formation of all habits is a feedback loop. Your values, principles and identity should drive the loop rather than your results. A habit is a behavior that has been repeated enough times to become automatic. The process of habit formation begins with trial and error. The process of building a habit can be divided into four simple steps cue, craving response and reward. This four-step pattern from the book "Atomic Habits" is the backbone of every habit and your brain runs through these steps in the same order each time.

Cue: - the cue triggers your brain to initiate a behavior. It is a bit of information that predicts a reward. Your mind is continuously analyzing your internal and external environment for hits of where rewards are located.

Craving: - is the motivational force behind every habit. With some level of motivation or desire, without craving for change, we have no reason to act. What you crave is not the habit itself, but the change in state it delivers. E.g., you do not crave smoking a cigarette, you crave the feeling of relief it provides.

Response: - is the actual habit you perform, which can take the form of thought or action. The response may depend on your motivation levels and the friction associated with the behavior. Response also depends on your ability; a habit can occur only if you are capable of doing it.

Reward: - Response delivers a reward, the end goal of every habit. The craving is about wanting the reward, response is about obtaining the reward. We chase rewards because they satisfy us and they teach us. If the behavior is insufficient in any of the four stages, it will not become a habit. Eliminate the cue, your habit will never start. Reduce the craving, and you won't experience enough motivation to act. And if the reward fails to satisfy your desire, then you will have no reason to do it again in the future.

Whenever you want to change your behavior, you can simply ask yourself

How can I make it obvious?

How can I make it attractive?

How can I make it easy?

How can I make it satisfying?

With enough practice, you can notice the cues that predict certain outcomes without consciously thinking about it. One of the most practical ways to eliminate a bad habit is to reduce exposure to the cue that causes it... People with high self-control tend to spend less time in tempting situations. It is easier to avoid temptation than resist it. Make it attractive, the more attractive an opportunity is, the more likely it is to become habit forming. It is the anticipation of rewards not the fulfilment of it that gets us to take action. The greater the anticipation, the greater the dopamine spike

The Importance of Building Habits in Personal Mastery

Consistency and Progress: Habits provide a framework for consistent actions, fostering incremental progress over time. In the journey of personal mastery, small, consistent actions compound to create significant positive changes.

Automaticity and Efficiency: Habits, once established, operate on autopilot, requiring less cognitive effort. This frees up mental resources, allowing individuals to focus on higher-order tasks and goals in their pursuit of personal mastery.

Stability in Transitions: Habits provide stability during times of change or transition. Whether returning from a sabbatical or navigating a career shift, well-established habits serve as a reliable anchor, promoting resilience and adaptability.

Components of Effective Habit Building

Identifying Keystone Habits: Keystone habits are

foundational behaviors that have a ripple effect on other areas of life. Identify keystone habits that align with personal mastery goals. Focusing on these habits can create a domino effect, positively impacting various aspects of your life.

Start Small and Gradual Progress: Starting with small, manageable habits is key to building sustainable routines. Break down larger goals into smaller, actionable steps. Gradual progress reduces overwhelm and increases the likelihood of habit formation.

Cue-Routine-Reward Loop: The habit loop consists of a cue (trigger), routine (habitual behavior), and reward (positive reinforcement). Identify cues that prompt your desired habits, establish a routine, and associate a reward to reinforce the behavior. This loop strengthens the habit over time.

The Role of Habit Building in Personal Development

Mindset Transformation: Habit building contributes to a mindset shift. As individuals consistently engage in positive habits, their mindset evolves, aligning more closely with the principles of personal mastery, growth, and continuous improvement.

Enhancing Discipline and Willpower: Habit building strengthens discipline and willpower. Through repeated practice, individuals develop the resilience to overcome challenges, setbacks, and the temptation to revert to old, less constructive habits.

Creating a Supportive Environment: Habits are influenced by environmental cues. Shaping your environment to support positive habits and minimize obstacles contributes to successful habit formation, facilitating personal mastery.

Strategies for Building Effective Habits

Set Clear Goals: Clearly define your personal mastery goals. Setting specific and measurable goals provides a roadmap for identifying the habits that will contribute to your overall development.

Build Habits Gradually: Introduce habits gradually to avoid overwhelm. Gradual habit-building increases the likelihood of long-term adoption. Starting with one or two habits allows for focused attention and increased success.

Track Progress: Use a habit tracker to monitor your progress. Tracking habits provides visibility into your consistency, highlights areas for improvement, and serves as positive reinforcement.

Accountability and Support: Share your goals with a friend or mentor. Having someone to hold you accountable and provide support can significantly increase your chances of building and sustaining positive habits.

Reflect and Adjust: Regularly reflect on your habits and adjust as needed. Life is dynamic, and habit effectiveness may change. Reflecting on your habits allows for continuous improvement and adaptation to evolving circumstances.

Building habits is a cornerstone of personal mastery, offering a structured and sustainable approach to achieving growth and development. By understanding the importance of habits, recognizing their components, and implementing effective strategies, individuals can harness the transformative power of intentional routines in their journey toward personal mastery.

Creating Powerful Habits

Creating powerful habits is a transformative process that requires intentional planning, consistent effort, and a commitment to personal growth. Here's a step-by-step guide to help you establish powerful habits in your life:

Get clear on your Goals and Values: Clearly identify your long-term goals and the values that align with them. Understanding the "why" behind your habits provides motivation and purpose.

Break Down Goals into Smaller Habits: Divide larger goals into smaller, manageable habits. Breaking them down makes the process less overwhelming and allows for incremental progress.

Start Small: Begin with small, achievable habits. Starting with small increases, the likelihood of success builds momentum for more significant changes over time.

Identify Grounding Habits: foundational behaviors that can have a positive impact on other areas of your life. Focusing on these habits can create a domino effect.

Establish Routine Loop: Design a habit loop with a cue (trigger), routine (habitual behavior), and reward. The reward reinforces the habit, creating a positive feedback loop.

Choose Consistent Cues: Select cues that are consistent and tied to existing routines. Integration with existing habits makes it easier to adopt new ones.

Be Specific: Clearly define the specifics of your habit. Specify when, where, and how you will perform the habit to make it more concrete.

Set a Trigger: Link your new habit to an existing habit to create a natural trigger. For example, if your existing habit is having morning coffee, make it a trigger for a morning stretching routine.

Schedule Regular Times: Set specific times for your habits. Consistency in timing helps in establishing a routine and reinforces the habit loop.

Use Reminders: Set reminders on your phone or use visual cues to prompt your habit. This helps maintain awareness and ensures you don't forget to perform the habit to perform the habit.

Track Your Progress: Keep a habit tracker or journal to monitor your progress. Tracking provides a visual representation of your consistency and helps identify patterns.

Seek Accountability: Share your goals with a friend, family member, or accountability partner. Having someone to check in with increases your commitment to the habit.

Remember, the key to creating powerful habits is consistency and perseverance. Start with small, manageable changes, and over time, these habits will become ingrained in your daily life, contributing to your overall personal mastery and well-being.

How will creating powerful habits help women on sabbatical get back to work

Creating powerful habits can significantly benefit women on sabbatical who are looking to re-enter the workforce. The transition from a career break to a professional setting can be challenging, but establishing positive habits can help ease the process and enhance your chances of success. Here's how powerful habits can assist women on sabbatical in returning to work:

Skill Enhancement: Cultivate a habit of continuous learning. Dedicate time each day or week to enhance your skills, whether through online courses, workshops, or networking events. Staying updated on industry trends and acquiring new skills will boost your confidence and make you more competitive in the job market.

Networking: Develop a habit of networking regularly. Attend industry events, join professional groups, and connect with professionals in your field on social media platforms like LinkedIn. Networking helps you stay informed about job opportunities, industry changes, and builds valuable connections that can support your return to work.

Resume and LinkedIn Optimization: Establish a routine for updating your resume and LinkedIn profile. Highlight your skills, achievements, and any new certifications or training you've acquired during your sabbatical. Keeping your professional documents up-to-date ensures you are ready to seize potential job opportunities.

Set Realistic Goals: Form the habit of setting achievable short-term and long-term career goals. Break down your goals into smaller, manageable tasks. This approach makes the process less overwhelming and allows you to track your progress effectively.

Job Search Routine: Create a habit of dedicating focused time to your job search. This includes researching job opportunities, customizing your applications, and practicing interview skills. A consistent job search routine increases your chances of finding suitable positions and securing interviews.

Self-Care: Prioritize self-care as a habit. Returning to work can be demanding, so it's crucial to take care of your physical and mental well-being. Regular exercise, sufficient sleep, and mindfulness practices can contribute to a positive mindset and increased resilience during the job search process.

Confidence Building: Develop habits that boost your confidence. This may include positive affirmations, visualization exercises, or seeking mentorship. Confidence is key during interviews and when re-entering the workforce after a sabbatical.

Flexibility and Adaptability: Cultivate the habit of being flexible and adaptable. The work landscape may have changed during your sabbatical, and being open to new ideas, technologies, and work arrangements will make your transition smoother.

Seek Support: Make it a habit to seek support from mentors, friends, or support groups. Sharing your experiences and challenges with others who have gone through a similar transition can provide valuable insights and encouragement.

Practice Interviewing: Dedicate time to practice common interview questions and refine your responses. Conduct mock interviews with a friend or mentor to build confidence and improve your communication skills.

Remember that re-entering the workforce is a process that takes time, and creating these powerful habits can help you navigate this journey more effectively. Stay persistent, be patient with yourself, and celebrate the small victories along the way.

Time Management

"Productivity is never an accident. It is always the result of a commitment to excellence, intelligent planning and focused effort."
- Paul J. Meyer

In the quest for personal and professional success, the art of time management stands tall, with goal setting and prioritization as its foundational pillars. This chapter explores how the deliberate establishment of goals and the strategic prioritization of tasks contribute to efficient time management, providing individuals with a roadmap to navigate the complexities of their lives.

Do you ever feel like there is not enough time in a day?

We all get the same 24 hours, so why do some people seem to achieve more with their time than others The answer is good time management.

Time management is the process of organizing and

planning how to divide your time between different activities. Get it right, and you will end up working smarter, not harder, to get more done in less time, even when time is tight and pressures are high.

The highest achievers manage their time exceptionally well. And by using Mind Tools and Time Management resources, you too can make the most of your time starting right now!

The Benefits of Good Time Management

When you know how to manage your time effectively, you can unlock many benefits. These include:

Greater productivity and efficiency.

Less stress.

A better professional reputation.

Increased chances of advancement.

More opportunities to achieve your life and career goals.

Overall, you start feeling more in control, with the confidence to choose how best to use your time. By feeling happier, more relaxed, and being able to think better, you are in a great place to help others reach their targets, too.

How do you effectively manage your time?

Start by assessing your existing situation. How good are you at organizing your time so that you get the important things done well? Can you balance your time between different activities? And when you do make time to do something, are you able to focus and get it finished?

Good time management takes a shift in focus from activities to results. Being busy is different from being effective. In fact, for many people, the busier they are, the less they actually achieve.

General Time Management Tools: Mind Tools has a range of resources designed to improve your time management overall. These offer solutions to common time management challenges, as well as ways to change key habits for the better.

Being More Organized explains why your environment needs to be as organized as your thinking. There are practical tips from highly organized people, plus ideas for using technology to take more control of your time. Good time management relies on planning, recording and reflecting on your activities.

Prioritization: You can achieve more when you start dedicating time to the right things. But how do you know what those things are? By identifying between demands, so that you prioritize them wisely. Exploring how much time to give to different activities if you should be doing them at all.

Scheduling: You may know what you need to do, but when should you do it? Timing is everything. It pays to get tough tasks done while you are still feeling fresh. You can boost your efficiency, gain people's trust, and use adrenaline to your advantage.

Goal Setting: The most successful time managers have clear targets to aim for. They develop S.M.A.R.T Goals, allowing them to allocate their time effectively. Mind Mapping is a powerful way to see your goals clearly so that you are motivated to give them the time they need. Personal Mission Statements are also helpful for being organized and staying committed to your plans.

Time management means organizing your time intelligently, so that you use it more effectively. The benefits of good time management include greater productivity, less stress, and more opportunities to do the things that matter. Being more organized, prioritize better, schedule tasks appropriately and complete work in a focused and efficient way. Having clear goals helps to guide your time management by helping you to stay motivated and disciplined. And also, on overcoming common time management challenges, so that you keep improving your approach and using your time to the full!

In the pursuit of personal mastery, one aspect stands out as a linchpin for success—time management. Time, the most finite resource available to us, holds the power to shape our lives and determine the trajectory of our personal development. This chapter explores the importance of time management within the context of personal mastery and delves into its essential components.

The Importance of Time Management

Time management is a critical skill that plays a pivotal role in personal and professional success. Effectively managing your time can have a profound impact on various aspects of your life, and its importance extends across different domains. Here are some key reasons why time management is essential:

Productivity and Efficiency: Time management allows individuals to prioritize tasks and allocate time to activities that contribute to their goals. This prioritization enhances productivity and efficiency, ensuring that time is spent on tasks that yield the most significant results.

Goal Achievement: Successful goal achievement is closely tied to effective time management. By setting clear goals and allocating time resources appropriately, individuals can make steady progress toward their objectives. Time management helps turn aspirations into actionable steps.

Reduced Stress: Poor time management often leads to procrastination, rushed work, and missed deadlines, contributing to heightened stress levels. When individuals manage their time effectively, they can approach tasks with a sense of control, reducing stress and anxiety associated with tight schedules.

Improved Decision Making: Time management involves prioritizing tasks based on their importance and deadlines. This process requires individuals to make decisions about how to allocate their time wisely. Over time, consistent decision-making in the context of time management leads to better overall decision-making skills.

Enhanced Focus and Concentration: Effective time management involves breaking tasks into manageable chunks and focusing on one task at a time. This approach enhances concentration and reduces the likelihood of distractions, ultimately leading to higher-quality work.

Work-Life Balance: Time management is crucial for maintaining a healthy work-life balance. By efficiently organizing work tasks and personal activities, individuals can dedicate time to both their professional and personal lives, preventing burnout and maintaining overall well-being.

Increased Opportunities: Time management allows individuals to identify and capitalize on opportunities. With a well-organized schedule, one can proactively seek out new projects, collaborations, or learning opportunities that align with their goals.

Personal Development: Time management is a key component of personal development. By allocating time to learning new skills, pursuing hobbies, or engaging in self-improvement activities, individuals can continuously grow and evolve.

Resource Optimization: Time is a finite resource, and effective time management ensures its optimal utilization. It helps avoid wasting time on unproductive activities, leading to a more efficient use of resources, both personal and organizational.

Long-Term Success: Consistent time management is a hallmark of individuals who achieve long-term success. It involves planning for the future, setting priorities, and making decisions that contribute to sustained growth and accomplishment.

Time management is a foundational skill that influences various aspects of an individual's life. Whether in the workplace, at home, or in personal pursuits, the ability to manage time effectively is a key factor in achieving success, reducing stress, and fostering a balanced and fulfilling life. Without the conscious allocation of time, the journey towards personal mastery becomes a chaotic expedition rather than a purposeful odyssey.

Components of Effective Time Management

At the heart of effective time management lies the ability to set clear goals and prioritize them based on their significance. Personal mastery requires a roadmap, and goal setting provides the milestones that guide individuals toward their desired destination. Prioritization ensures that time is allocated to activities that align with overarching objectives, preventing distractions from derailing the journey.

The Significance of Goal Setting

Defining Clear Objectives: Goal setting is the compass that guides our actions and decisions. Clearly defined objectives serve as the destination on our journey, providing a sense of purpose and direction. In the realm of time management, setting specific, measurable, achievable, relevant, and time-bound (SMART) goals becomes the first step toward harnessing the power of time effectively.

Motivation and Commitment: Goals fuel motivation and commitment. When individuals set goals that resonate with their values and aspirations, they are more likely to stay focused and committed. This section delves into the psychological impact of setting meaningful goals, exploring how they become the driving force behind intentional time management.

Breaking Down Long-Term Goals: Long-term goals may seem daunting, but breaking them down into smaller, actionable steps makes them more manageable. This section provides strategies for dissecting ambitious objectives into achievable tasks, ensuring that individuals can make consistent progress without feeling overwhelmed.

The Art of Prioritization

The Urgent vs. Important Matrix: Effective time management requires a keen understanding of what is urgent and what is important. The Urgent vs. Important Matrix, popularized by Stephen Covey, has become a valuable tool for categorizing tasks. This section explains how prioritizing based on urgency and importance helps individuals focus on what truly matters.

Identifying High-Impact Activities: Not all tasks are created equal. Prioritization involves recognizing high-impact activities that align with overarching goals. This section guides individuals in identifying tasks that contribute significantly to their success, allowing them to allocate time and energy where it matters most.

Flexibility in Prioritization: While planning is crucial, life is unpredictable. This section emphasizes the importance of flexibility in prioritization. It explores strategies for adapting to unexpected changes, shifting priorities when necessary, and maintaining focus on the most critical tasks amid evolving circumstances.

Integrating Goal Setting and Prioritization

Aligning Tasks with Goals: Effective time management requires a seamless integration of goal setting and prioritization. This section provides practical tips on aligning daily tasks with overarching goals, ensuring that each action contributes to the realization of desired outcomes.

Creating Daily and Weekly Plans: Building on the principles of goal setting and prioritization, this section explores the creation of daily and weekly plans. It emphasizes the importance of scheduling tasks, allocating time strategically, and establishing routines that foster consistency in time management.

Reflection and Adjustment: No time management strategy is static. Regular reflection on goals and priorities allows individuals to assess their progress, identify areas for improvement, and make necessary adjustments. This section encourages a dynamic approach to time management, ensuring continued alignment with evolving aspirations.

Mastering Time Through Purposeful Planning

In the tapestry of time management, goal setting and prioritization emerge as threads that, when woven together with intentionality, create a fabric of purpose and accomplishment. As individuals embark on their journey of mastering time, the fusion of clear objectives and strategic prioritization becomes the compass that not only guides them through the present but also propels them toward a future rich with fulfillment and success.

The Essence of Planning

Setting the Stage with Clear Objectives: At the heart of effective planning lies a clear understanding of one's objectives. This section emphasizes the importance of defining short-term and long-term goals, exploring how a well-defined destination informs the journey and serves as the North Star guiding daily planning efforts.

Creating Actionable Plans: Effective planning involves translating goals into actionable plans. This section delves into the art of breaking down larger objectives into smaller, manageable tasks. It explores methodologies such as the breakdown of tasks into milestones, creating to-do lists, and leveraging project management tools to ensure a structured approach.

Incorporating Time Blocking Techniques

Time blocking, a strategic planning technique, involves dedicating specific blocks of time to particular activities. This section explores how time blocking enhances focus and productivity, providing individuals with a visual representation of their day and preventing the pitfalls of multitasking.

The Symphony of Organization

Digital and Physical Organization Strategies: Organization extends beyond planning; it involves creating systems to manage information and tasks efficiently. This section discusses the importance of both digital and physical organization, exploring how tools such as calendars, task management apps, and physical organizers contribute to a streamlined approach.

Decluttering the Workspace and the Mind: An organized workspace is a reflection of an organized mind. This section delves into the benefits of decluttering both physical and mental spaces, creating an environment conducive to focus and productivity. It explores techniques for minimizing distractions and maintaining a clear, uncluttered mindset.

Establishing Routines and Rituals: Consistency is a hallmark of effective organization. This section explores the power of routines and rituals, illustrating how they create a sense of structure and predictability. By incorporating rituals into daily and weekly schedules, individuals can streamline tasks and optimize their time.

Integration and Continuous Improvement

Seamless Integration of Planning and Organization: The true power of planning and organization lies in their seamless integration into daily life. This section explores how individuals can integrate planning and organizational strategies into their routines, creating a harmonious balance that supports efficient time management.

Reflection for Continuous Improvement: No plan is flawless, and no system is immune to evolution. Regular reflection becomes a vital component of continuous improvement. This section encourages individuals to reflect on their planning and organizational strategies, identify areas for enhancement, and adapt their approaches to align with changing circumstances.

Success through Purposeful Planning and Organization: As individuals navigate the intricate dance of time management, the melodies of planning and organization provide the rhythm that propels them forward. Together, these skills orchestrate a symphony of productivity and success, ensuring that each note resonates with purpose. By mastering the art of planning and organization, individuals not only streamline their daily activities but also lay the foundation for a future rich with achievement and fulfillment.

Execution and Adaptability

Execution: Execution is the bridge between planning and achievement. Effective time management involves not only envisioning a path but also taking deliberate steps to traverse it. Execution requires discipline, focus, and a commitment to the allocated timeframes. Personal mastery is built on consistent action, and effective time management transforms plans into tangible results.

Adaptability: While planning is crucial, life is inherently unpredictable. The ability to adapt to unforeseen circumstances without compromising long-term goals is a hallmark of successful time management. Personal mastery thrives when individuals can navigate challenges, adjust their schedules, and maintain resilience in the face of change.

Reflection and Continuous Improvement

A key component often overlooked in discussions about time management is reflection. Regularly assessing how time is spent, identifying areas of improvement, and celebrating successes are integral to the process of personal mastery. Continuous improvement is fueled by self-awareness, and reflection provides the insights necessary to refine time management strategies, ensuring they remain aligned with evolving personal goals.

Time management is the compass that guides individuals on their journey towards personal mastery. By embracing the importance of goal setting, planning, execution, adaptability, and reflection, individuals can navigate the complexities of their lives with intentionality and purpose. As time becomes an ally rather than a constraint, the pursuit of personal mastery transforms into a transformative and fulfilling odyssey.

How will time management help women on sabbatical get back to work

Time management plays a crucial role in helping women on sabbatical successfully transition back into the workforce. Returning to work after a break requires careful planning, efficient use of time, and the cultivation of habits that facilitate a smooth reintegration. Here's how time management can be beneficial, along with practical steps to achieve it:

Skill Enhancement: Allocate specific time slots for skill enhancement activities. Set aside dedicated hours each week for updating your skills. This can include online courses, workshops, and networking events. By managing your time effectively, you ensure a consistent focus on skill development.

Networking and Industry Engagement: Schedule regular networking sessions and industry engagement activities. Block time on your calendar for attending networking events, industry conferences, and online webinars. Regularly check and respond to professional messages on platforms like LinkedIn during designated time slots.

Job Search and Application Process: Create a structured job search routine. Dedicate specific hours each day or week to search for job openings, customize your applications, and follow up on submissions. A focused and organized approach to job searching saves time and increases the effectiveness of your efforts.

Confidence Building: Schedule regular sessions for confidence-building activities. Set aside time for activities that boost your confidence, such as practicing interview scenarios, seeking mentorship, or engaging in positive affirmations. Consistent effort in these areas can enhance your self-assurance over time.

Adaptability and Flexibility: Include adaptability in your planning. Recognize that unexpected events may disrupt your schedule. Build flexibility into your time management strategy to accommodate changes without derailing your overall plan. This adaptability is vital during a period of transition.

Reflection and Adjustment: Regularly reflect on your progress and adjust your plan accordingly. Set aside time periodically to assess your job search strategy, skill development, and overall progress. Reflecting on what is working and making adjustments ensures that you stay on track and continue to refine your approach.

By incorporating these time management strategies into their routine, women on sabbatical can efficiently balance the various aspects of returning to work. The key is to be intentional about how time is spent and to create a schedule that aligns with personal and professional goals. Through effective time management, the transition back into the workforce becomes a more organized and successful endeavor.

9

Mindfulness and Spirituality

Being on a spiritual path does not prevent you from facing times of darkness. But it teaches you how to use the darkness as a tool to grow.

In the pursuit of personal mastery, the integration of spirituality and mindfulness acts as the nurturing soil for the seeds of growth. This chapter embarks on a soulful journey, exploring the profound importance of spirituality and mindfulness in the quest for self-discovery, purpose, and holistic well-being.

At its core, spirituality transcends religious affiliations, encompassing a profound connection with the self, others, and the universe. This section delves into the essence of spirituality as a deeply personal and transformative force that contributes to the tapestry of personal mastery. It encompasses a holistic approach to personal development that goes beyond the material and external aspects of life.

Here are key elements that define the essence of spirituality in the context of personal mastery:

- Connection with the Inner Self

- Mindfulness Practices
- Interconnectedness and Unity
- Empathy and Compassion
- Search for Higher Meaning and Purpose
- Alignment with Values
- Inner Peace and Harmony
- Balance and Harmony
- Transcendence of Ego and Materialism
- Detachment from Materialism
- Continuous Growth and Learning
- Integration of Wisdom
- Service to Others and Contribution
- Social and Environmental Responsibility
- Embracing Mystery and Transcendence
- Accuracy of Limiting Beliefs

Spirituality in personal mastery is a transformative journey that integrates self-discovery, interconnectedness, purposeful living, inner peace, and continuous growth. It provides a profound framework for navigating life's challenges, cultivating meaningful relationships, and contributing to the well-being of oneself and the broader community.

The Core of Spirituality in Personal Mastery

Connecting with Higher Purposes: Spirituality often involves seeking meaning beyond the tangible aspects of life. This section explores the role of spirituality in connecting individuals with higher purposes, fostering a sense of purpose that goes beyond personal success to contribute to the greater good. It's about seeking a sense of purpose, fulfillment, and contribution that resonates with a broader, often transcendent, understanding of existence.

Here's a breakdown of what it means to connect with higher purposes in the context of personal mastery:

Exploration of Meaning and Significance

Reflecting on Life's Purpose: Connecting with higher purposes begins with contemplation and self-reflection on the meaning and purpose of one's life. This involves asking profound questions about existence, values, and the contribution one wishes to make to the world.

Seeking Significance: Individuals on the path of personal mastery actively seek significance in their actions and choices. They strive to understand how their endeavors contribute to a greater whole and make a positive impact on themselves and others.

Alignment with Core Values

Identifying Core Values: Connecting with higher purposes requires a clear understanding of one's core values. These values serve as guiding principles that influence decisions, behaviors, and the overall direction of life.

Living in Alignment: Individuals committed to personal mastery align their actions and choices with their core values. This alignment brings a sense of integrity and authenticity, ensuring that daily decisions are congruent with the deeper values that guide them.

Contributing to the Greater Good: Connecting with higher purposes often involves a commitment to service. Individuals recognize their capacity to contribute positively to the well-being of others and actively seek opportunities to make a meaningful difference in the lives of those around them.

Social and Environmental Responsibility: Higher purposes extend beyond individual concerns to encompass social and environmental responsibility. Personal mastery involves a sense of duty to contribute to the collective well-being and the sustainability of the planet.

Transcendence of Self-Centered Goals: Individuals pursuing personal mastery recognize the limitations of self-centered goals and ambitions. Connecting with higher purposes involves transcending narrow self-interest and embracing a broader perspective that considers the well-being of the community and the world. This may involve participation in social causes, advocating for positive change, or contributing talents and resources to initiatives that promote the common good.

Striving for Excellence and Growth: Connecting with higher purposes involves a commitment to continuous personal growth. Individuals on the path of personal mastery understand that their development contributes to their ability to make a more profound impact on the world. Pursuing higher purposes often entails striving for excellence in all endeavors. This commitment to excellence reflects a dedication to making a meaningful and positive contribution to the broader context in which one lives and works.

Finding Meaning in Challenges and Adversities: Individuals connected with higher purposes approach challenges and adversities with resilience and purpose. Rather than viewing setbacks as obstacles, they see them as opportunities for growth and learning on the journey toward personal mastery.

Turning Setbacks into Opportunities: Adversities become platforms for individuals to demonstrate their commitment to higher purposes. They use setbacks as catalysts for positive change and transformation, understanding that the path to personal mastery is marked by both successes and challenges.

Cultivating a Transcendent Perspective: Connecting with higher purposes often involves embracing a transcendental perspective on life. This could be expressed through spiritual beliefs, a sense of awe and wonder, or a recognition of the interconnectedness of all things.

Mind-Body-Spirit Harmony

Spirituality is not confined to the ethereal it extends to the physical and mental realms. This section highlights the importance of achieving harmony between the mind, body, and spirit, creating a holistic foundation for personal mastery. It involves cultivating a holistic approach to personal development, acknowledging the interconnectedness of the mind, body, and spirit, and fostering a sense of equilibrium and alignment among these dimensions.

Here's a breakdown of what Mind-Body-Spirit Harmony entails in the context of personal mastery:

Mental Harmony (Mind)

Cognitive Clarity: Mental harmony involves achieving clarity of thought and cognitive awareness. It includes practices such as mindfulness, meditation, and self-reflection to quiet the mind, enhance focus, and promote mental clarity.

Emotional Intelligence: Individuals in pursuit of Mind-Body-Spirit Harmony cultivate emotional intelligence. This involves understanding and managing one's emotions, empathizing with others, and fostering positive relationships, contributing to a harmonious mental state.

Positive Mindset: Maintaining a positive mindset is crucial for mental harmony. It involves adopting an optimistic outlook, reframing challenges as opportunities, and cultivating resilience in the face of adversity.

Physical Harmony (Body)

Physical Well-being: Achieving physical harmony involves prioritizing and maintaining physical well-being.

This includes regular exercise, a balanced diet, sufficient rest, and adequate hydration to support overall health and vitality.

Mindful Movement Practices: Incorporating mindful movement practices, such as yoga or tai chi, contributes to physical harmony. These practices not only enhance flexibility and strength but also foster a mind-body connection, promoting overall wellness.

Restorative Practices: Recognizing the importance of rest and recovery is essential for physical harmony. Incorporating practices like adequate sleep and relaxation techniques allows the body to rejuvenate and maintain a state of balance.

Spiritual Harmony (Spirit)

Alignment with Core Values: Spiritual harmony involves aligning one's actions and choices with core values and beliefs. It includes seeking a sense of purpose, living authentically, and integrating spiritual principles into daily life.

Connection with the Sacred: Individuals pursuing Mind-Body-Spirit Harmony often seek a connection with the sacred or a higher power. This may involve spiritual practices, prayer, meditation, or engagement with meaningful rituals that nurture the spirit.

Transcendence and Transcendent Experiences: Spiritual harmony includes moments of transcendence—experiences that go beyond the ordinary and connect individuals to something greater than themselves. This may involve awe, wonder, or a sense of oneness with the universe.

Integration and Balance

Holistic Awareness: Achieving Mind-Body-Spirit Harmony requires holistic awareness. This involves recognizing the interplay between mental, physical, and spiritual dimensions and understanding how each aspect contributes to overall well-being.

Balancing Priorities: Individuals in pursuit of harmony prioritize activities and practices that contribute to mental, physical, and spiritual wellness. They strike a balance between work, personal life, and self-care, ensuring that no single dimension dominates at the expense of others.

Adaptability: Maintaining harmony involves adaptability. Individuals recognize that the balance between mind, body, and spirit may shift in response to life's changes and challenges, and they cultivate the flexibility to adjust their practices accordingly.

Mind-Body-Spirit Practices

Holistic Practices: Engaging in holistic practices that address the mind, body, and spirit simultaneously fosters harmony. Examples include meditation, mindfulness, holistic therapies, and integrative health approaches that consider the interconnectedness of well-being.

Mindful Eating: Mindful eating is a practice that embodies Mind-Body-Spirit Harmony. It involves paying attention to the sensory experience of eating, making conscious food choices, and recognizing the connection between nutrition and overall well-being.

Mind-Body-Spirit Retreats: Participating in retreats or immersive experiences that integrate mental, physical, and spiritual practices provides an opportunity for deepening harmony. These retreats often offer a supportive environment for self-discovery and holistic growth.

Importance of Spirituality and Mindfulness in Personal Mastery

Inner Peace and Resilience: In the dynamic landscape of personal mastery, inner peace and resilience are invaluable assets. This section explores how spirituality and mindfulness contribute to cultivating a serene inner landscape and building resilience in the face of life's challenges.

Clarity of Purpose and Values: Spirituality often involves a journey of self-discovery, leading to a deep understanding of personal values and purpose. This section explores how clarity in purpose and values, nurtured through mindfulness practices, becomes a compass guiding individual toward personal mastery.

Enhanced Emotional Intelligence: Mindfulness fosters emotional intelligence by encouraging individuals to observe their thoughts and emotions without judgment. This section examines how heightened emotional intelligence, supported by spiritual insights, enhances interpersonal relationships and personal effectiveness.

Components of Spiritual and Mindful Practices

Meditation and Contemplation: Central to both spirituality and mindfulness, meditation and contemplation serve as foundational practices. This section explores various meditation techniques and contemplative practices that individuals can incorporate into their daily routines.

Mindful Breathing and Body Awareness: Conscious breathing and body awareness form pillars of mindfulness. This section guides individuals in the practice of mindful breathing and tuning into the sensations of the body, fostering a connection between the physical and spiritual realms.

Gratitude and Compassion Practices: Gratitude and compassion are integral aspects of spiritual and mindful living. This section explores practices that cultivate gratitude and compassion, elevating the individual's perspective and fostering a sense of interconnectedness.

Integrating Spirituality and Mindfulness into Daily Life

Morning and Evening Rituals: Creating rituals infused with spiritual and mindful elements bookends the day with intention. This section offers insights into establishing morning and evening rituals that set the tone for mindfulness and spiritual connection.

Mindful Eating and Savoring: Eating mindfully is a practice that extends spiritual awareness to daily sustenance. This section explores the significance of mindful eating and savoring each moment, turning meals into opportunities for gratitude and presence.

Silence and Solitude: Amidst the noise of modern life, carving out moments of silence and solitude becomes a sanctuary for spiritual and mindful practices. This section delves into the transformative power of embracing silence and solitude for personal reflection and growth.

Overcoming Challenges on the Spiritual Path

Navigating Doubt and Uncertainty: The spiritual journey is not without its challenges. This section addresses common doubts and uncertainties that individuals may encounter on their spiritual path and offers guidance on navigating these challenges with resilience.

Balancing Spirituality and Practical Realities: In the pursuit of personal mastery, balancing spiritual pursuits with practical realities is essential. This section provides insights into integrating spiritual practices into a busy life, emphasizing the harmony between spiritual exploration and pragmatic responsibilities.

Cultivating a Lifelong Journey of Personal Mastery

Embracing the Ever-Unfolding Journey: The integration of spirituality and mindfulness is not a destination but a lifelong journey. This section encourages individuals to view personal mastery as an ever-unfolding process, inviting continuous growth, self-discovery, and the deepening of spiritual and mindful practices.

Building a Supportive Community: A sense of community can enrich the spiritual and mindful journey. This section explores the importance of connecting with like-minded individuals, whether through spiritual groups, mindfulness workshops, or other avenues, to share insights, experiences, and mutual support.

Sustaining the Flame of Personal Mastery: It emphasizes the cyclical nature of spiritual and mindful practices, encouraging individuals to revisit and refine their approaches, fostering a sustained commitment to the transformative journey of personal mastery.

How spirituality, mindfulness and meditation help women on sabbatical get back to work

Embarking on the journey back to work after a sabbatical can be both exciting and challenging. Incorporating spirituality, mindfulness, and meditation into this transition can provide valuable tools for self-discovery, stress reduction, and enhanced focus.

Here's how these practices can help women on sabbatical get back to work and some practical steps to achieve it:

Reducing Stress and Anxiety: Practice Mindfulness Meditation; Engage in mindfulness meditation to reduce stress and anxiety. Mindfulness helps cultivate a non-judgmental awareness of the present moment, allowing you to manage the uncertainties and pressures associated with returning to work.

Building Confidence and Self-Awareness: Take time for spiritual reflection to gain insights into your strengths, values, and aspirations. This self-awareness contributes to increased confidence as you re-enter the workforce, providing a clearer understanding of your unique contributions.

Enhancing Focus and Concentration: Mindful Breathing Exercises; Incorporate mindful breathing exercises to enhance focus and concentration. Simple breathing techniques can help calm the mind, improve mental clarity, and prepare you for the demands of a work environment.

Cultivating Resilience: Draw on spiritual practices, such as prayer or affirmations, to cultivate resilience. Connecting with your spiritual beliefs can provide a sense of purpose and strength, helping you navigate challenges with a positive mindset.

Setting Realistic Goals: Use mindfulness techniques to set realistic and achievable goals. Mindful goal setting involves breaking down larger objectives into smaller, manageable steps, allowing for a gradual and successful reintegration into the workforce.

Improving Communication Skills: Mindful Communication Practices; Practice mindful communication to improve interpersonal skills. Mindful listening and thoughtful expression can enhance your ability to communicate effectively with colleagues, superiors, and clients.

Managing Time Effectively: Apply mindfulness to time management. Prioritize tasks mindfully, allocate time intentionally, and avoid multitasking. This approach helps in maintaining focus and efficiency during work-related activities.

Cultivating a Positive Mindset: Embrace spiritual affirmations to foster a positive mindset. Affirmations aligned with your spiritual beliefs can serve as powerful tools for cultivating optimism, resilience, and a can-do attitude as you transition back to work.

Staying Grounded During Transitions: Mindful Grounding Techniques; During moments of stress or change, employ mindful grounding techniques. These may include connecting with your breath, focusing on sensory experiences, or practicing mindfulness exercises that anchor you in the present moment.

Networking and Building Relationships: Leverage spiritual communities or groups to expand your network. Attend relevant events or join groups that align with your spiritual beliefs. Networking within these circles can provide a supportive environment as you navigate professional connections.

Balancing Work and Personal Life: Mindful Work-Life Integration; Integrate mindfulness into your work-life balance. Set boundaries, prioritize self-care, and be mindful of the need for both professional and personal fulfillment. Mindfulness practices can help you maintain equilibrium in the face of competing demands.

Continuous Learning and Adaptability: Spiritual Growth Mindset; Approach the return to work with a growth mindset influenced by your spiritual beliefs. Embrace continuous learning and view challenges as opportunities for personal and professional growth.

Practical Steps to Achieve Spiritual and Mindful Integration

Create a Sacred Space: Designate a quiet and inspiring space for your spiritual and mindfulness practices. This could be a corner in your home or a specific location that fosters a sense of tranquility.

Establish a Daily Routine: Develop a daily routine that includes time for spiritual reflection, mindfulness meditation, and any other practices that resonate with you. Consistency is key to reaping the benefits of these practices.

Seek Guidance: Explore resources, books, or workshops that align with both your spiritual beliefs and mindfulness goals. Seeking guidance from experienced practitioners can deepen your understanding and enhance your practice.

Join Supportive Communities: Connect with spiritual and mindfulness communities. Attend local or online groups where you can share experiences, gain insights, and receive support during your transition back to work.

Incorporate Mindfulness into Daily Activities

Infuse mindfulness into your daily activities, such as eating, walking, or commuting. Being present in these moments enhances your overall mindfulness and contributes to a more centered and focused mindset.

Set Intentional Breaks: During your workday, set intentional breaks for brief mindfulness exercises. This could include a mindful breathing exercise, a short walk, or a moment of gratitude to recenter and recharge.

Utilize Mindfulness Apps: Explore mindfulness apps that offer guided meditations, breathing exercises, and daily mindfulness reminders. These tools can be valuable companions in integrating mindfulness into your daily life.

Attend Mindfulness Workshops: Consider attending workshops or courses on mindfulness and meditation. These sessions may provide additional techniques and insights to enhance your practice and apply mindfulness to various aspects of your life.

Journaling and Reflection: Maintain a journal for spiritual reflections and mindfulness observations. Journaling can serve as a powerful tool for self-discovery, tracking progress, and capturing moments of insight during your sabbatical transition.

Build a Support System: Share your spiritual and mindfulness journey with supportive friends, family, or mentors. Having a supportive system can provide encouragement, guidance, and a sense of connection during your return to work.

Practice Self-Compassion: Be kind to yourself as you navigate the challenges of returning to work. Practice self-compassion, recognizing that the journey may have its ups and downs, and that personal mastery is a continuous process.

Spirituality, mindfulness, and meditation can be powerful allies for women on sabbatical seeking a harmonious return to work. By integrating these practices into daily life, cultivating self-awareness, and fostering a positive mindset, women can navigate the transition with resilience, purpose, and a sense of inner balance.

As individuals embark on the transformative journey of personal mastery, the integration of spirituality and mindfulness emerges as the paintbrush that unveils the masterpiece within. By nurturing the soul and cultivating a mindful presence, individuals not only discover profound depths within themselves but also navigate the complexities of life with grace and purpose. The chapter concludes by inviting readers to embark on their unique journey, where spirituality and mindfulness intertwine to create a canvas of personal mastery that reflects the beauty of the soul.

10

Self-Regulation

"Self-regulation is about looking non-judgmentally at one's impulses, worries and fixations." **- Dr. Stuart Shanker**

Self-Regulation

Self-regulation refers to the ability to manage and control one's thoughts, emotions, behaviors, and impulses in a purposeful and adaptive manner. It involves the capacity to regulate one's internal states, responses, and actions in alignment with personal goals, values, and social norms. Self-regulation encompasses a set of cognitive, emotional, and behavioral processes that enable individuals to navigate various situations, make constructive decisions, and maintain a sense of balance and well-being.

Key components of self-regulation include emotional regulation, cognitive control, and the capacity to modify or inhibit one's behavior in accordance with established standards or objectives. Overall, self-regulation plays a crucial role in achieving long-term goals, fostering resilience, and contributing to effective interpersonal relationships.

The thread of self-regulation weaves through every aspect of one's journey. This chapter delves into the profound importance of self-regulation, exploring its role as a guiding force in navigating challenges, fostering resilience, and achieving a harmonious balance in the pursuit of personal mastery. Self-regulation is a dynamic process that evolves in response to different situations and challenges. This section delves into the adaptive nature of self-regulation, emphasizing its role in fostering flexibility and resilience in the face of life's ever-changing landscape.

Components of Self-Regulation

Emotional Self-Regulation: Emotional self-regulation is a cornerstone of personal mastery. This section explores the importance of understanding and managing one's emotions, highlighting techniques such as mindfulness, self-awareness, and emotional intelligence as essential components of emotional self-regulation. Emotional self-regulation is a fundamental aspect of personal mastery, encompassing the ability to understand, manage, and adapt one's emotional responses in various situations. It plays a crucial role in fostering emotional intelligence, maintaining mental well-being, and navigating the complexities of personal and professional life.

Emotional self-regulation involves the ability to recognize, understand, and modulate one's own emotions. It includes managing the intensity, duration, and expression of emotions in a way that aligns with personal goals and social expectations. The foundation of emotional self-regulation lies in self-awareness. Individuals on the path of personal mastery actively observe and acknowledge their emotional states, recognizing the triggers and patterns that influence their feelings.

Importance of Emotional Self-regulation in Personal Mastery

Enhanced Decision-Making: Emotional self-regulation contributes to more rational and thoughtful decision-making. By managing impulsive emotional reactions, individuals can make choices aligned with their long-term goals and values.

Resilience and Adaptability: In the pursuit of personal mastery, resilience is essential. Emotional self-regulation fosters resilience by enabling individuals to bounce back from setbacks, learn from experiences, and adapt to changing circumstances.

Improved Relationships: Emotional intelligence, a byproduct of emotional self-regulation, enhances interpersonal relationships. The ability to understand and regulate one's emotions contributes to effective communication, empathy, and the building of meaningful connections.

Mindfulness Practices: Mindfulness involves being fully present in the moment, observing thoughts and emotions without judgment. Mindful practices, such as meditation and mindful breathing, are effective for cultivating emotional self-regulation.

Overcoming Challenges in Emotional Self-Regulation

Identifying Triggers: Recognizing emotional triggers is crucial. Personal mastery involves understanding the specific situations or thoughts that elicit strong emotional responses, allowing individuals to proactively manage these triggers.

Continuous Learning: Emotional self-regulation is an ongoing process of learning and refinement. Individuals on the path of personal mastery view challenges as opportunities for growth and learning, continuously improving their emotional regulation skills.

Seeking Support: During challenging times, seeking support from friends, mentors, or mental health professionals can be valuable. Sharing emotions and receiving guidance contributes to emotional self-regulation and personal growth.

Workplace Effectiveness: Emotional self-regulation is critical in the workplace. It enables individuals to handle stress, communicate effectively, and collaborate with colleagues, contributing to a positive and productive work environment.

Conflict Resolution: In personal and professional relationships, emotional self-regulation is essential for effective conflict resolution. It allows individuals to express themselves calmly, listen empathetically, and find mutually beneficial solutions.

Well-Being and Life Satisfaction: Emotional self-regulation is closely linked to overall well-being and life satisfaction. Individuals who can navigate their emotions skillfully experience a greater sense of contentment and fulfillment.

Emotional self-regulation is a cornerstone of personal mastery, empowering individuals to navigate the complex landscape of emotions with grace and intention. By understanding, accepting, and effectively managing their emotional responses, individuals on the journey of personal mastery cultivate resilience, make informed decisions, and build meaningful connections with themselves and others. Through continuous practice and a commitment to self-awareness, emotional self-regulation becomes a transformative force, shaping the path toward a more fulfilling and purpose-driven life.

Cognitive Self-Regulation

Cognitive self-regulation involves managing one's thoughts, attention, and cognitive processes. This section delves into the role of cognitive restructuring, positive self-talk, and cognitive flexibility in cultivating a mindset that aligns with personal mastery goals. Cognitive self-regulation in personal mastery involves the intentional control and management of cognitive processes, thoughts, and mental activities to achieve specific goals, enhance well-being, and optimize overall cognitive functioning. This aspect of self-regulation is crucial for individuals seeking personal mastery as it influences decision-making, problem-solving, and the development of a positive mindset.

Importance of Cognitive Self-regulation in Personal Mastery

Positive Mindset: Cognitive self-regulation is integral to maintaining a positive mindset. Individuals on the path to personal mastery actively regulate negative thoughts, reframe challenges as opportunities, and cultivate a belief in their ability to learn and grow.

Decision-Making: Sound decision-making is a cornerstone of personal mastery. Cognitive self-regulation enables individuals to approach decision-making with clarity, weighing pros and cons, considering long-term consequences, and aligning choices with personal values.

Problem-Solving: Effective problem-solving is enhanced by cognitive self-regulation. Individuals can approach problems systematically, break them down into manageable components, and generate creative solutions, fostering a sense of mastery over challenges.

Strategies for Cognitive Self-Regulation

Mindfulness Practices: Mindfulness enhances cognitive self-regulation by promoting focused attention and awareness of thoughts. Mindfulness meditation and other mindfulness practices help individuals observe and regulate their cognitive processes.

Cognitive Restructuring: Cognitive restructuring involves identifying and challenging negative or irrational thoughts. Individuals practice replacing unhelpful thought patterns with more constructive and positive alternatives.

Goal Setting and Planning: Cognitive self-regulation is closely tied to goal setting and planning. Individuals set clear, achievable goals and develop strategic plans, breaking down larger objectives into smaller, manageable tasks.

Overcoming Challenges in Cognitive Self-Regulation

Awareness of Cognitive Biases: Individuals practicing cognitive self-regulation actively work to identify and mitigate cognitive biases that may impact their thinking. This awareness helps them make more objective and informed decisions.

Building Cognitive Resilience: Cognitive resilience involves bouncing back from setbacks and adapting to challenges. Individuals with strong cognitive self-regulation skills view failures as opportunities for learning and growth, fostering resilience.

Continuous Learning: Personal mastery involves a commitment to continuous learning. Individuals regularly seek new information, perspectives, and skills, fostering cognitive flexibility and adaptability.

Cognitive self-regulation is a cornerstone of personal mastery, influencing the way individuals think, learn, and navigate challenges. By actively managing their cognitive processes, individuals can cultivate a positive mindset, make informed decisions, and adapt to the ever-changing landscape of personal and professional life. Through mindfulness, cognitive restructuring, and a commitment to continuous learning, cognitive self-regulation becomes a powerful tool for achieving personal mastery and unlocking one's full potential.

Behavioral Self-Regulation

Behavioral self-regulation focuses on aligning actions with intentions and values. This section explores strategies for developing discipline, setting goals, and cultivating habits that support personal growth. It also addresses the challenges of breaking undesirable habits and establishing positive routines. Behavioral self-regulation in personal mastery involves the intentional control and modification of one's actions, habits, and responses to external stimuli. It is a crucial aspect of self-discipline and goal attainment, contributing to the overall journey of personal development and mastery.

Let's explore the key components, strategies, and significance of behavioral self-regulation in the context of personal mastery:

Components of Behavioral Self-Regulation

Goal Setting: Behavioral self-regulation begins with setting clear, specific, and achievable goals. Individuals identify what they want to accomplish, breaking down larger objectives into smaller, manageable steps.

Impulse Control: Successful behavioral self-regulation requires the ability to control impulses and resist immediate gratification in favor of long-term goals. This involves making deliberate choices rather than reacting impulsively to stimuli.

Establishing Routines: Creating and adhering to routines helps in maintaining consistency. Behavioral self-regulation involves establishing positive daily habits that contribute to personal growth, well-being, and the achievement of goals.

Importance of Behavioral self-regulation in Personal Mastery

Habit Formation: Behavioral self-regulation is instrumental in habit formation. Individuals consciously cultivate positive habits that support their journey toward personal mastery, replacing undesirable behaviors with constructive ones.

Consistency in Action: Personal mastery requires consistent effort over time. Behavioral self-regulation ensures that individuals consistently act in alignment with their values and goals, contributing to sustained progress and growth.

Adaptability: As individuals encounter challenges and changing circumstances, behavioral self-regulation allows for adaptability. Individuals can adjust their behaviors and strategies, overcoming obstacles and staying on course toward personal mastery.

Strategies for Behavioral Self-Regulation

Self-Monitoring: Regular self-monitoring involves tracking behaviors, progress, and adherence to goals. This awareness allows individuals to identify patterns, celebrate successes, and make necessary adjustments to stay on track.

Reward Systems: Implementing a reward system reinforces positive behaviors. Individuals set up incentives for achieving milestones, creating a motivational framework that encourages continued behavioral self-regulation.

Visualization: Visualization involves mentally rehearsing successful behaviors and outcomes. By vividly imagining the desired actions and results, individuals enhance their commitment to behavioral self-regulation and reinforce a positive mindset.

Overcoming Challenges in Behavioral Self-Regulation

Identifying Triggers: Recognizing triggers that lead to undesired behaviors is crucial. Individuals develop awareness of situations, emotions, or environmental cues that may prompt unwanted actions, allowing them to proactively address these triggers.

Building Resilience: Behavioral self-regulation involves building resilience to setbacks. Individuals understand that occasional lapses are a natural part of the process and use setbacks as opportunities to learn, adjust, and strengthen their resolve.

Seeking Social Support: Engaging in a supportive community or seeking accountability partners can enhance behavioral self-regulation. Sharing goals and progress with others creates a network of encouragement and reinforces commitment.

Behavioral self-regulation is a cornerstone of personal mastery, providing individuals with the tools to consciously shape their actions and behaviors. By setting and pursuing meaningful goals, resisting impulses, and establishing positive habits, individuals foster discipline, consistency, and adaptability in their journey toward personal growth and mastery. Through self-monitoring, resilience-building, and the cultivation of supportive environments, behavioral self-regulation becomes a transformative force, propelling individuals toward the realization of their full potential.

Cultivating Self-Regulation Strategies

Mindfulness and Meditation Practices: Mindfulness and meditation are potent tools for enhancing self-regulation. This section provides practical insights into incorporating mindfulness and meditation into daily routines, emphasizing their impact on emotional balance and cognitive clarity.

Goal Setting and Planning Techniques: Effective goal setting and planning are essential components of behavioral self-regulation. This section explores goal-setting strategies, such as SMART goals, and emphasizes the importance of creating realistic action plans to support sustained self-regulation.

Developing Emotional Intelligence: Emotional intelligence is a key facet of emotional self-regulation. This section explores strategies for developing emotional intelligence, including self-awareness, self-management, social awareness, and relationship management.

Self-Regulation helps in Overcoming Challenges by:

Identifying Common Challenges: Even the most adept individuals face challenges in self-regulation. This section identifies common obstacles such as procrastination, impulsivity, and self-doubt. It provides insights into recognizing and overcoming these challenges on the journey to personal mastery.

Building a Support System: A supportive environment enhances self-regulation. This section explores the role of community, mentors, and accountability partners in bolstering self-regulation efforts. It emphasizes the power of collaboration and shared experiences in overcoming challenges.

Continuous Improvement and Adaptability: Self-regulation is an ongoing process of refinement. This section encourages individuals to view setbacks as opportunities for learning and growth, emphasizing the importance of adaptability and a growth mindset in mastering the art of self-regulation.

Embracing Self-Regulation as a Lifelong Companion

As individuals embark on the transformative journey of personal mastery, self-regulation emerges as a steadfast companion, guiding them through the peaks and valleys of growth. This concluding section underscores the enduring importance of self-regulation, encouraging readers to embrace it not as a rigid discipline but as a dynamic and evolving force that empowers them to shape their destinies with intention, resilience, and a profound sense of mastery.

How will self-regulation help women on sabbatical get back to work

Self-regulation plays a crucial role in helping women on sabbatical get back to work by providing a framework for managing various aspects of their personal and professional lives. Here's how self-regulation can be beneficial and some strategies to achieve it:

Time Management: Effective time management is vital for women returning to work after a sabbatical. Self-regulation helps in prioritizing tasks, setting realistic goals, and managing time efficiently.

- Create a schedule or daily plan to allocate time for work-related activities, personal responsibilities, and self-care.
- Use time-blocking techniques to focus on specific tasks during designated periods.
- Set realistic deadlines for tasks and projects to avoid feeling overwhelmed.

Emotional Self-Regulation: Returning to work may bring about various emotions such as excitement, anxiety, or uncertainty. Emotional self-regulation is essential for managing these feelings and maintaining a positive mindset.

- Practice mindfulness and relaxation techniques to stay centred and reduce stress.
- Acknowledge and validate emotions, but also challenge negative thoughts and replace them with positive affirmations.
- Seek support from mentors, colleagues, or counsellors to discuss concerns and gain perspective.

Networking and Relationship Building: Building and maintaining professional relationships is crucial for a successful return to the workforce. Self-regulation aids in effective communication and relationship management.

- Set goals for networking, such as attending industry events, connecting with colleagues on professional platforms, and scheduling informational interviews.
- Use active listening skills to understand the perspectives of others and communicate effectively.
- Join professional groups or associations related to your field to expand your network.

Skill Development and Continuous Learning: Self-regulation supports ongoing skill development, enabling women to stay competitive in their field and adapt to changes in the workplace.

- Identify relevant skills for your industry and set specific goals for acquiring or enhancing them.
- Enrol in online courses, attend workshops, or participate in training programs to stay updated on industry trends.
- Create a personalized learning plan and allocate time regularly for skill development.

Confidence Building: Self-regulation contributes to building and maintaining confidence, which is crucial for re-entering the workforce after a sabbatical.

- Set achievable goals that gradually increase in complexity to build a sense of accomplishment.
- Celebrate small successes and milestones to reinforce confidence.
- Practice positive self-talk and challenge self-doubt by focusing on past achievements.

Work-Life Integration: Achieving a balance between work and personal life is essential for overall well-being. Self-regulation helps in setting boundaries and maintaining this balance.

- Clearly define work hours and personal time and communicate these boundaries with colleagues and family.
- Prioritize self-care activities and allocate time for relaxation and rejuvenation.
- Regularly assess and adjust the balance based on personal and professional needs.

Flexibility and Adaptability: The ability to adapt to changes in the workplace and industry is crucial. Self-regulation fosters flexibility in navigating uncertainties.

- Embrace a growth mindset, viewing challenges as opportunities for learning and development.
- Stay informed about industry changes and be open to acquiring new skills as needed.
- Develop a plan for handling unexpected situations and be adaptable in adjusting goals and strategies.

Setting Realistic Expectations: Self-regulation helps in setting realistic expectations for oneself, reducing the likelihood of feeling overwhelmed or experiencing burnout.

- Break down larger goals into smaller, manageable tasks to maintain a sense of control.

- Regularly reassess goals and adjust them based on changing circumstances.
- Prioritize tasks and focus on the most important and time-sensitive activities.

Seeking Support and Mentorship: Self-regulation involves recognizing when to seek support from others. Mentorship can provide guidance and insights for a successful return to work.

- Identify mentors or advisors who can offer guidance on career decisions and professional development.
- Seek feedback from colleagues and supervisors to gain insights into performance and areas for improvement.
- Build a support network of individuals who understand the challenges of returning to work after a sabbatical.

Building a Routine: Establishing a routine helps in creating a sense of structure and stability, making the transition back to work smoother.

- Create a daily and weekly routine that includes work tasks, personal commitments, and self-care activities.
- Stick to a consistent schedule to enhance productivity and reduce stress.
- Adjust the routine as needed based on feedback and changing circumstances.

By incorporating these strategies and fostering self-regulation in various aspects of life, women on sabbatical can enhance their readiness and confidence as they transition back to the workforce. It's important to recognize that the return to work is a gradual process, and self-regulation provides a valuable framework for navigating challenges and maximizing personal and professional success.

Strategy for Transformation

11

Unraveling your Life's Purpose

"Light your life with purpose and all shadows will disappear."
- Gillian Duce

What is the Purpose of Life?

As I reflect upon the journey of my life, I find myself standing at a crossroads where the path I have been traveling seems to diverge from the essence of my existence. It's a realization that unfolds gradually, like the pages of a book revealing a story I never thought I would write. In the quiet moments of introspection, I began to sense a disconnection from my purpose, prompting me to embark on a quest to rediscover the meaning of my life.

The first inkling of my deviation came as a subtle whisper in the midst of routine. The days blurred into one another, and the once vibrant colors of passion began to fade into shades of monotony. I found myself going through the motions without truly feeling the pulse of my purpose. A discomfort settled in my heart, and I couldn't ignore the nagging question that echoed in the recesses of my mind: For what am I really living?

As I grappled with this existential inquiry, I became acutely aware of the need to explore the very fabric of my being. Purpose, I realized, is not a fixed destination but a dynamic journey that evolves with our growth. It's a compass that guides us, yet its true nature eluded me. Was it a career, relationships, or something more profound that would fill the void within?

In my search for purpose, I delved into the wisdom of philosophers, poets, and thinkers who sought to unravel the enigma of human existence. Their words became stepping stones on my path, guiding me through the maze of self-discovery. Slowly, I began to understand that purpose is not a singular entity but a mosaic of passion, values, and contributions that define our individual narratives.

I found myself drawn to activities that resonated with my core values and beliefs. The joy I derived from these endeavors felt like a gentle nudge from the universe, guiding me back to the essence of who I am. Purpose, it seemed, was not an external pursuit but an internal alignment with the authentic self.

As the layers of distraction peeled away, I confronted the uncomfortable truth that I had allowed external expectations to cloud my vision. Society's definitions of success and fulfillment had overshadowed the unique melody of my own calling. The pursuit of purpose, I realized, required a daring rebellion against conformity and a courageous embrace of individuality.

I was on the abyss of a new beginning. The journey to rediscover my purpose has been both a reckoning and a revelation. I've learned that purpose is not a fixed point but a dance with the rhythm of life. As I step into the next chapter, I carry with me the lessons learned, armed with a newfound clarity about the meaning of my existence. The search for purpose, I now understand, is not a destination but an ongoing dialogue between my heart and the universe.

Finding purpose in life adds psychological and emotional improvements and satisfaction to life. There is a want for more zest, more flavor, more fullness. In the strictest sense, you want to become a better person.

Think of uncovering your passion like the work of a master sculptor, slowly chipping away the stone to reveal the masterpiece underneath. Your life's purpose is this masterpiece, simply hiding beneath the surface, waiting to be released. The fastest way to learn how to find your purpose is through the art of introspection, diving into the deeper essence of who you are to pull out the pieces to assemble the purpose puzzle.

Think of your life's purpose as a golden thread; for some, that thread comes in the form of a certain career or profession, while for others, it looks like a way of being or expression. Your purpose can be the driving force behind this. If you feel lost, your sense of purpose can be your connection to something larger, something that will allow you to truly make a difference.

To get clarity on it, answer this question:

Why do you want to find your purpose in life?

Write down whatever comes to mind. It might be some of the above reasons, or it might be something entirely different. Whatever it is, hold it close.

Have you ever woken up in a dark room with no source of light at all? Did you manage to do anything worthwhile? That's how living a life without a clear purpose is. The majority of people live their lives in this manner. You need to find your purpose to have a meaningful life.

What purpose means

The concept of purpose is a multifaceted and deeply philosophical idea that encompasses various dimensions of human existence. While interpretations may vary, purpose generally refers to the reason for which something exists or is done. In the context of individual human lives, purpose involves a sense of direction, meaning, and significance.

Here are some key aspects of what purpose means:

Meaning and Significance: Purpose gives meaning to our actions and experiences. It provides a framework for understanding why we do what we do and why certain things matter to us. Without purpose, life may feel devoid of significance, leading to a sense of emptiness or aimlessness.

Direction and Focus: Purpose serves as a guiding force that directs our decisions, goals, and actions. It helps us prioritize what is truly important to us and align our efforts with our core values. With a clear sense of purpose, individuals are better equipped to make choices that contribute to their overall well-being and fulfillment.

Passion and Motivation: Purpose is often intertwined with passion. When we discover activities, causes, or pursuits that align with our purpose, a deep sense of motivation and enthusiasm follows. Passion fuels our commitment, resilience, and willingness to invest time and effort into endeavors that resonate with our sense of purpose.

Contribution to Others: For many, purpose extends beyond personal fulfillment and includes a desire to contribute to the well-being of others or society at large. Acts of kindness, service, and making a positive impact are often integral components of a purpose-driven life.

Alignment with Values: Understanding one's purpose involves an exploration of personal values and beliefs. Purposeful living requires aligning one's actions and choices with these core values, fostering a sense of authenticity and integrity.

Personal Growth and Fulfillment: Purpose is closely linked to personal growth and self-realization. As individuals strive to live in accordance with their purpose, they often embark on a journey of self-discovery, continuously evolving and expanding their capacities for joy, fulfillment, and inner harmony.

Connection to a Larger Whole: Some conceptualize purpose as being part of a larger cosmic or existential framework. This perspective suggests that individuals are connected to something greater than themselves, and finding purpose involves understanding and embracing this connection.

Evolutionary Nature: Purpose is not static; it evolves over time. As individuals grow, learn, and adapt to changing circumstances, their understanding of purpose may shift. Embracing this evolutionary nature allows for a dynamic and flexible approach to living a purposeful life.

Purpose is a deeply personal and subjective aspect of human experience. It involves introspection, self-discovery, and a continuous exploration of what brings meaning and fulfillment to one's life.

How finding purpose can help you improve the quality of your life:

1. Think about what makes you Look for a Life Purpose?

You didn't just pick this book aimlessly. You were intrigued. Your interest has kept you reading this far. You can't say it was a coincidence or a meaningless read.

On the surface, picking this book was a random act. But that is not actually how your mind works. Sit down and think about the trail that led you to this point.

Here are simple starting points to help you find your life purpose.

What made you want to know more about your life's purpose?

What triggered your mind to pay attention to this issue?

What are some things that you don't find as exciting in your life?

What things have sparked joy in your life recently?

2. Having a Purpose Makes Life Meaningful

Your purpose is the reason you get up every morning and can lead to better relationships and improved physical health. Life without a clear purpose can get boring and unsatisfying. Once you find and understand your purpose, your life will never be the same again.

You will start attracting things you have always wanted into your life. You will have health, wealth, and peace of mind. Remember, everything starts from within. Your outer world is a clear reflection of your inner world.

A purposeless life will always achieve fear, worry, and poverty. Since you want to live a meaningful life, pay attention to your thinking patterns and set aside a few daily minutes to find and clarify your purpose.

3. You will have a deeper understanding of yourself

We all think that we know ourselves. But only a few understand themselves on a deeper level. Knowing yourself will help you gain confidence and improve the quality of your life.

You will realize your outstanding characteristics and hidden talents as you work towards your true purpose. In this process, you will acknowledge your strengths and weaknesses.

By accepting yourself the way you are and doing

everything in your power to improve yourself, you'll attract adventure and confidence into your life.

4. You will challenge your limiting beliefs

Purpose always arises from a deep desire for a specific situation. And in most cases, whom you aspire to become may be far from the life you are living right now.

Due to this, you'll find yourself questioning if your purpose can materialize in your life with all the resources and skills you lack right now. The purpose is so powerful because it challenges you in a good way.

It will help you develop or improve your skills and find the needed resources. Reframing your limiting beliefs is all you need to do to transform your life. As I said earlier, your outer world reflects your inner world. Therefore, you need to discover your purpose.

HOW TO FIND PURPOSE IN LIFE

I came to the conclusion after a lot of research on finding purpose is that purpose changes as per the situations of life for example for a hungry jobless person, his purpose will be to get next meal, for a sick person would be to get better and live his life normally. Same way, we cannot fixate on one single thing forever. Under any situation focusing on what is that we like do live for should be the purpose. There are many benefits of knowing your purpose, but how can you figure it out? It is a combination of the science of achievement and the art of fulfilment that creates the road to happiness and a life of meaning. To succeed in finding your purpose, you must master this balance.

1. Search Inward

You can never truly understand how to find your purpose by listening to others' opinions and seeking outside approval.

Everything you need is within yourself. The only thing holding you back is your own limiting beliefs. With each limiting belief you identify and replace with an empowering belief, you develop greater self-awareness. When you are in control of your emotions, you are in control of your life.

2. Put Purpose before Goals

If you focus only on achieving short-term goals, you will never find your true passion or learn how to find your purpose. The goals you work toward must always be based on finding your purpose. If they are not, you will only feel a fleeting sense of accomplishment and will soon be seeking something more. You won't be able to see that life is happening for you instead of to you.

When you set a goal, ask yourself: How will this help me feel more fulfilled? How does this relate back to my purpose? Using a journal helps to keep you focused on your purpose

3. Focus on what you have

Developing an abundance mindset is like opening your eyes to life, you will see beauty and goodness all around you. With this new perspective, your purpose in life becomes much clearer. You question less and less how to find your purpose because you feel like you have more of the answers and that you are on the path to achieving meaningful goals.

When we focus on what we have, fear disappears and abundance appears. You will stop living in fear that you are wasting your life and begin to attract positivity and joy. Finding your purpose becomes an exciting journey, rather than a stressful goal.

4. Taking Ownership of your life

True fulfilment comes from designing your own life. This is how you unlock the extraordinary. To find your purpose, you must decide what's truly right, and know it in your heart and soul. You must not let yourself be driven by fear or anxiety. A decision made from fear is always the wrong decision. It will not help you understand "What is my purpose?" but instead it will confuse the issue even more.

To take ownership, you must stop playing the victim. Realize that every circumstance in your life is a result of your own decisions, not anyone else's. When you take responsibility for finding your purpose instead of blaming others, fulfilment follows.

5. Think about what brings you joy

Look back on your life's journey so far and identify the times when you felt the most joy. Was it when you were connecting with your friends? Making a successful presentation at work? Creating art or helping others? When you discover what brings you joy, you usually discover where your passions lie.

Your abilities are connected to that sense of joy, so examine them, can you pick up a pencil and sketch a lifelike portrait? Do your friends tell you that you are a great listener? When you look closely at the activities or skills that come naturally and also bring you joy, you will likely stumble upon passions that you can turn into a profitable career.

6. Develop your own life vision statement

Before you can ask yourself "What is my purpose?" you first have to know what an ideal world looks like and how you fit into it. Creating a life vision statement involves identifying what life would look like if everyone were living up to their fullest potential. This will help you develop a roadmap to guide you in the proper direction.

7. Discover your true needs

Some people don't even know where to start. If you fall into this category, it helps to examine these human needs, which are certainty, significance, variety, love/connection, growth or contribution which affects every decision you make.

Lack of awareness about your own needs can leave you with a false sense of purpose, one that is actually based on others' expectations. This is why you can reach the top of the career ladder, find the "perfect" partner or be in the best shape of your life, but still not feel happy. Fulfilment begins with your innermost needs.

8. Write out your story

Writing helps us organize our thoughts and discover new ones we may not even know we had. It is proven to help us reach goals, improve memory and decrease stress, which are all essential when you are learning how to find your purpose.

Putting your life in writing can reveal hidden meanings you may not see otherwise. Start with answering these - What strengths do you have that helped you get through tough times? How have you helped others? And how have other people helped you? Write it all down and you will begin to see patterns that will help you find your purpose.

9. Take time for yourself

"What is my purpose?" is a deep question that takes time and reflection to answer. When you spend all your time running from one commitment to another, you never have time to just sit quietly and reconnect with yourself. Make sure you schedule enough personal time to reduce the noise and demands of the outer world and focus on what you want.

When you feel depleted searching for meaning in life, take a deep breath and centre yourself. Take time for self-care, whether that is a spa day or reading a book or just a stroll in the park. It is by looking within that you are able to identify your values and the beliefs you hold most dear as a guiding force in life. You won't understand how to find your purpose without first taking a step back and relaxing.

10. Embrace acceptance

Part of finding your purpose is accepting your own limitations. Instead of getting frustrated with yourself, give yourself a break. Get to know yourself bit by bit, taking the role of observer. As you practice self-compassion while building self-awareness, you are able to find the meaning you are seeking.

Self-compassion means being patient with yourself. Feeling lost in life can be a very disorienting feeling. You may feel frustrated, but be gentle with yourself. Everyone who has ever asked themselves "What is my purpose?" began from a place of uncertainty. Their hesitancy was what prompted them to dig deep and find greater meaning.

Finding your purpose is a lifelong journey. Being flexible lets you grow in integrity while being true to yourself. When you develop your core values and stop seeking external affirmation, you will find that the question of "What is my purpose in life?" is much easier to answer.

Why is it important to identify one's purpose

Identifying one's purpose is crucial for several reasons, and the significance of this process extends across various aspects of an individual's life.

Here are some key reasons why it is important to identify one's purpose:

Provides Meaning and Direction: Understanding one's purpose gives life a sense of meaning and direction. It answers the fundamental question of "Why am I here?" and provides a compass that guides decisions, goals, and actions. Without a clear sense of purpose, individuals may feel lost or unfulfilled.

Guides Decision-Making: Purpose serves as a valuable guide in decision-making. When faced with choices, having a clear understanding of one's purpose helps prioritize options that align with personal values and long-term objectives. This can lead to more intentional and fulfilling life choices.

Fosters Intrinsic Motivation: A life driven by purpose is often accompanied by a strong sense of intrinsic motivation. Engaging in activities that resonate with one's purpose brings a deep sense of satisfaction and passion, fueling the drive to pursue goals with enthusiasm and perseverance.

Enhances Well-Being: Living a purposeful life is associated with higher levels of psychological well-being. Studies suggest that individuals who have a sense of purpose experience lower levels of stress, anxiety, and depression. Purpose contributes to a positive outlook on life and a greater overall sense of happiness.

Promotes Resilience in the Face of Challenges: When individuals have a strong sense of purpose, they are often more resilient in the face of adversity. Knowing why they are pursuing certain goals or facing challenges provides a source of strength and determination during difficult times.

Fosters Personal Growth and Development: Identifying one's purpose often involves a journey of self-discovery and personal growth. It encourages individuals to explore their strengths, values, and interests, fostering continuous development and evolution as they align their lives with their authentic selves.

Builds a Foundation for Goal Setting: Purpose provides a foundation for setting meaningful and fulfilling goals. Goals that are aligned with one's purpose are more likely to be pursued with dedication and sustained effort, leading to a greater sense of achievement.

Strengthens Interpersonal Relationships: Knowing one's purpose can enhance relationships with others. Shared values and aligned purposes can strengthen connections, whether in personal relationships, friendships, or collaborative efforts. It creates a sense of unity and shared vision.

Contributes to a Positive Impact on Society: For many individuals, purpose extends beyond personal fulfillment to include a desire to contribute positively to society. People with a clear sense of purpose often engage in activities that make a difference in the lives of others, contributing to the greater good.

Encourages a Life of Integrity: Living in accordance with one's purpose promotes a sense of integrity. It involves aligning actions with values, leading to a more authentic and honest way of life. This alignment fosters a sense of coherence and harmony within oneself.

Identifying one's purpose is essential for personal fulfillment, well-being, and a life that is lived with intention and authenticity. It serves as a guiding force that shapes the choices individuals make and the paths they pursue, contributing to a more meaningful and purpose-driven existence.

How to discover, work towards achieving and sustaining your purpose

Discovering, working towards achieving, and sustaining your purpose is a dynamic and personal journey.

Working towards Achieving Your Purpose

Set Clear Goals: Break down your purpose into actionable and measurable goals. What specific steps can you take to align your life with your purpose? Set short-term and long-term goals.

Create a Plan: Develop a plan outlining how you will achieve your goals. This could include acquiring new skills, building relationships, or making lifestyle changes. A well-thought-out plan provides direction and focus.

Build a Support System: Surround yourself with

supportive individuals who share similar values or have achieved similar goals. Their encouragement and guidance can be invaluable on your journey.

Embrace Challenges: Challenges are inevitable on the path to fulfilling your purpose. View them as opportunities for growth and learning. Resilience in the face of challenges is a key component of success.

Celebrate Milestones: Acknowledge and celebrate your achievements along the way. Recognizing your progress will keep you motivated and reinforce your commitment to your purpose.

Sustaining Your Purpose

Adapt and Evolve: Recognize that your purpose may evolve over time. Be open to adapting your goals and plans as you grow and learn more about yourself.

Practice Mindfulness: Regularly check in with yourself through mindfulness practices. This can help you stay connected to your purpose and ensure that your actions align with your values.

Cultivate Resilience: Develop resilience to navigate setbacks and challenges. Remember that setbacks are a natural part of any journey, and they provide opportunities for learning and growth.

Continuous Learning: Stay curious and committed to continuous learning. The more you learn, the more insights you'll gain into yourself and the world, further refining your understanding of your purpose.

Give Back: Consider how you can contribute to others and the community. Acts of service and giving back can deepen your connection to your purpose and create a positive impact on the lives of others.

Remember, the journey to discovering and sustaining your purpose is a lifelong process. It's okay if your understanding of your purpose evolves; what matters is the authenticity and commitment you bring to the exploration of your life's meaning.

Components of finding Purpose

The process of finding purpose is complex and multifaceted, involving various components that contribute to a deeper understanding of one's values, passions, and goals.

Here are key components involved in finding purpose:

Self-Reflection: Engaging in self-reflection is a fundamental component of finding purpose. It involves introspection, exploring your values, beliefs, strengths, weaknesses, and what truly matters to you. Reflecting on your life experiences and the things that bring you joy and fulfillment can provide valuable insights.

Identifying Values: Understanding your core values is crucial to finding purpose. What principles and beliefs are most important to you? Aligning your purpose with your values ensures that your life is congruent with what matters most to you.

Passions and Interests: Exploring your passions and interests is key to discovering purpose. What activities or subjects captivate your attention and make you feel alive? Passion often provides a compass for guiding your journey towards purpose.

Strengths and Talents: Recognizing your strengths and talents is essential. What are you naturally good at? How can you leverage your unique abilities to contribute to the world and find fulfillment in your endeavors?

Meaningful Experiences: Reflect on significant life experiences that have shaped you. Identify moments when you felt a deep sense of purpose or fulfillment. These experiences can offer valuable clues about the activities or pursuits that resonate with your authentic self.

Impact and Contribution: Consider the impact you want to have on others or the world. How do you want to contribute? Purpose often involves making a positive difference, whether on a personal, community, or global level.

Goal Setting: Setting specific, measurable, achievable, relevant, and time-bound (SMART) goals is a practical component of finding purpose. What steps can you take to align your life with your purpose? Establishing clear goals provides a roadmap for your journey.

Adaptability: Recognize that the discovery of purpose is an ongoing process, and it may evolve over time. Be adaptable and open to revisiting and refining your understanding of purpose as you grow and encounter new experiences.

Service and Contribution: Purpose often involves contributing to something larger than oneself. Consider how your skills, talents, and passions can be used to benefit others. Acts of service and contribution can deepen your connection to purpose.

By integrating these components into your life, you can embark on a holistic journey of self-discovery and purpose. Remember that finding purpose is a dynamic process, and the components may interact and influence each other throughout your life.

Connecting with heart of your Purpose

Connecting with the heart of your purpose involves delving deep into your core values, passions, and motivations. It's about creating a profound and authentic relationship with the essence of why you do what you do.

Here are steps to help you connect with the heart of your purpose:

1. Go with-in

Quiet the Noise: Set aside time for introspection. Find a quiet space where you can reflect without distractions. Silence external influences to listen to your inner voice.

Journaling: Write down your thoughts, feelings, and aspirations. Journaling allows you to explore your inner landscape, uncovering hidden desires and insights about your purpose.

2. Recognize Core Values

Values Exploration: Clarify your core values. What principles and beliefs are most important to you? Identify the values that resonate at the deepest level and align them with your purpose.

Prioritization: Once you've identified your values, prioritize them. Understand which values hold the greatest significance and how they contribute to shaping your purpose.

3. Explore Passions

Passion Mapping: Make a list of activities, causes, or subjects that ignite your passion. What makes your heart beat faster? These passions often hold the key to your purpose.

Past Joyful Experiences: Reflect on past experiences that brought you immense joy. What were you doing during those moments? Connecting with joyful experiences can reveal clues about your purpose.

4. Define Your "Why"

Purpose Statement: Craft a purpose statement that succinctly captures the essence of why you do what you do. This statement should reflect your values, passions, and the impact you want to make.

Dig Deeper: Continuously ask yourself "why" to dig

deeper into the layers of your motivation. Understanding the root cause of your actions brings clarity to your purpose.

5. Mindful Practices

Mindfulness Meditation: Practice mindfulness to stay present and connected to your inner self. Mindful meditation can help you become more aware of your thoughts and emotions related to your purpose.

Heart-Centered Meditation: Engage in heart-centered meditation to focus your attention on the emotions and sensations in your heart space. This practice fosters a deeper connection to your emotional core.

6. Visualizations

Future Self Visualization: Envision your future self-living in alignment with your purpose. Picture the positive impact you are making and the fulfillment you experience. Visualization can reinforce your connection to your purpose.

Symbolic Representations: Create symbols or visual representations of your purpose. This could be a vision board, a meaningful object, or an artistic expression that embodies the heart of your purpose.

7. Emotional Check-ins

Regular Reflection: Schedule regular check-ins with yourself. Reflect on how your actions and decisions align with your purpose. Adjust your course if needed, staying true to your heartfelt convictions.

Emotional Resonance: Pay attention to how certain activities or choices make you feel. If something resonates deeply with your heart, it's likely connected to the core of your purpose.

8. Seek Inspiration

Inspiring Stories: Read or listen to stories of individuals who have connected with the heart of their purpose. Their journeys can inspire and provide insights into your own path.

Mentorship: Seek guidance from mentors who have a strong connection to their purpose. Their experiences and wisdom can offer valuable perspectives on the journey to heartfelt purpose.

9. Continuous Learning and Adaptation

Curiosity: Stay curious and open to learning. The more you explore, experience, and adapt, the deeper your connection to the heart of your purpose can become.

Flexibility: Understand that your purpose may evolve. Be flexible and willing to adapt as you gain new insights and as your life circumstances change.

Connecting with the heart of your purpose is an ongoing, evolving process. It requires deep self-awareness, continuous exploration, and a commitment to living authentically. As you strengthen this connection, your purpose becomes a guiding force that shapes your decisions, actions, and overall life journey.

How having a purpose will help women on sabbatical get back to work

Having a clear sense of purpose can significantly aid women returning to the workforce after a sabbatical. Here are several ways in which having a purpose can be beneficial in this context:

1. **Renewed Motivation and Focus:** A well-defined purpose reignites passion and enthusiasm. Women returning from a sabbatical with a clear sense of purpose are likely to approach work with renewed motivation and focus. Purpose-driven individuals are often more intrinsically motivated. This internal drive can help women overcome challenges and

setbacks, maintaining their commitment to career reentry.

2. **Enhanced Confidence:** Having a purpose provides a clear direction. Women with a sense of purpose are more likely to project confidence, knowing where they want to go and what they want to achieve. It helps individuals recognize the value they bring to the workplace. Confidence in their skills and contributions can empower women to navigate the reentry process with self-assurance.
3. **Alignment with Personal Values:** Purpose often aligns with personal values. This alignment guides decision-making, making it easier for women to choose roles and opportunities that resonate with their core beliefs. Understanding one's purpose allows women to prioritize work in a way that aligns with their values, helping to maintain a healthy work-life balance.
4. **Effective Networking and Collaboration:** Purpose-driven individuals tend to connect more effectively with others who share similar values and goals. This can facilitate networking and collaboration during the reentry process. A clear purpose contributes to a shared vision within teams. Women returning to work can leverage their purpose to collaborate with colleagues, fostering a sense of unity and shared objectives.
5. **Continuous Learning and Adaptability:** Purpose-driven individuals are often committed to continuous learning and growth. Women returning to work after a sabbatical may demonstrate a proactive approach to acquiring new skills and adapting to changes in the workplace. Purpose fosters resilience. Facing the transition back to work can be challenging, but

a strong sense of purpose provides a foundation for navigating uncertainties and bouncing back from setbacks.

6. **Impactful Communication:** Women with a clear purpose can effectively communicate their stories. Sharing the journey of their sabbatical and the renewed commitment to their purpose makes for a compelling narrative that resonates with potential employers. Purpose-driven individuals often bring authenticity to their interactions. This authenticity can be a powerful asset during job interviews, creating a genuine connection with hiring managers.
7. **Time Management and Prioritization:** Knowing one's purpose facilitates effective time management. Women returning to work can prioritize tasks that align with their purpose, optimizing productivity, helping individuals balance various responsibilities by prioritizing activities that contribute to their overarching goals, allowing for a more organized and focused approach.
8. **Positive Mental Well-Being:** Having a purpose contributes to a sense of fulfillment. Women returning to work with a purpose are more likely to experience job satisfaction, positively impacting their mental well-being. Purpose provides a source of resilience during stressful periods. It serves as a grounding force, helping women navigate workplace challenges with a positive mindset.
9. **Contribution to Organizational Culture:** Purpose-driven individuals contribute positively to organizational culture. Women reentering the workforce bring a sense of purpose that can enhance team dynamics and overall workplace culture. Demonstrating a strong sense of purpose can inspire

colleagues and subordinates. Women with a clear purpose may become role models for others seeking purpose and fulfillment in their careers.

10. **Long-Term Career Planning:** Purpose guides long-term career planning. Women returning to work with a purpose are likely to make strategic decisions that align with their overall career objectives. Purpose provides a framework for adapting career trajectories based on changing life circumstances. Women can navigate their careers more intentionally, considering the alignment of their purpose at each stage.

Having purpose is a powerful asset and driving force for women returning to work after a sabbatical. It provides direction, motivation, and a sense of fulfillment that can positively influence various aspects of their professional journey. The clarity and resilience that come with a defined purpose can empower women to navigate challenges and contribute meaningfully to their work and the workplace culture.

Having a purpose in life is akin to discovering the North Star that guides us through the vast expanse of our existence. It is the compass that not only provides direction but also infuses our journey with meaning, passion, and resilience. A life with purpose transcends the mundane, offering a profound connection to our values, aspirations, and the greater tapestry of humanity. It serves as a source of motivation during challenges, a beacon of clarity in times of uncertainty, and a wellspring of joy in our accomplishments. Embracing and pursuing our purpose is a transformative journey, leading to a life lived with intention, authenticity, and a deep sense of fulfillment. As we navigate the complexities of our human experience, purpose becomes the narrative thread that weaves the story of our lives into a tapestry of significance and impact.

12

Zen Zone – The Art of Meditation

"Meditation is a way for nourishing and blossoming the divinity within you."

The Transformative Power of Meditation

Meditation, an ancient practice that has stood the test of time, is not merely a technique but a profound journey inward. In a world bustling with constant activity and external demands, the art of meditation emerges as a sanctuary for the mind and soul. This chapter delves into the importance of meditation, unraveling its transformative potential and exploring the fundamental components that make it a cornerstone of holistic well-being.

Meditation as a Lifestyle

Making meditation a lifestyle involves embracing mindfulness as a fundamental aspect of daily existence. It transcends being a mere practice and evolves into a way of being. It begins by establishing a consistent routine, setting aside dedicated time each day to engage in meditation. Creating a designated space for introspection reinforces the commitment to this lifestyle, signaling to the mind that moments of stillness and presence are essential. Integration is key, weaving mindfulness into the fabric of everyday activities, such as mindful walking, eating, or even commuting. Embracing various meditation techniques allows for flexibility and adaptation to different situations. Technology can be harnessed mindfully, using meditation apps or guided sessions to support the practice. Group meditation sessions and community involvement further anchor meditation as a social and communal aspect of life. As mindfulness permeates routine tasks, decision-making, and interactions, it shapes a mindset that appreciates the present moment and fosters resilience in the face of life's challenges. Choosing mindfulness as a lifestyle is an ongoing journey, a commitment to self-awareness, and a conscious effort to live each moment with intention and presence.

Meditation will calm your mind and help you reject the initial instinct to go off the road. It will help you to respond better in provocative situations.

Now that we are up to speed on why it is important to meditate, let's get to the hard part - the how.

Many people view meditation as something you need to do with the help of a Shaman, but the truth is you can do it on your own.

Once you master how to meditate properly on your own, the next step would be working it into your daily routine.

Meditation as a Daily ritual

There are so many suggestions on how best to meditate but that is not our focus. It doesn't have to be perfect; it doesn't have to be on the level of the sages or the ancient

Buddha. Here we are just going to discuss practical steps to developing a daily meditation habit or a ritual.

This way, you never forget and you are always aware when it is time to meditate.

Choose a method

Now that you have worked your way to the point of actual meditation, what's the next step? How exactly do I meditate?

There are an infinite number of meditation methods to choose from.

Here are a few basics ones to choose from:

Breath Control

Breath control is one of the most popular meditation methods. As you breathe in, try to empty your mind and follow the flow of air all the way from your nostrils to your lungs.

You could do this by counting also, whichever works for you. Try to pass on any thought that occurs during this process, just observe and let it go.

Visualization

This is another popular meditation method. Close your eyes and imagine a place that you love to be in or that is associated with peace and beauty.

Observe as many details as possible that bird, the sounds of flowing rivers, and the sound of wind hitting the leaves, the sound of rain imagine all of it. These details matter in meditation.

Create the most beautiful place that you can imagine and remain there throughout your meditation session.

Guided Meditation

Guided meditation usually involves a trained instructor or

teacher. The best part about guided meditation is you can do it anywhere. You don't have to join a class.

You can check out some instruction videos on YouTube, Amazon Prime, Audible and even Spotify. There are many great options and some of them are free!

Meditation Apps

For those of us who like to use our phones for everything, this one is for you.

With Meditation apps like Calm, Plum Village, Core Meditation, Headspace, YogaGlo and Insight Timer, you can meditate on the go.

Be Consistent

The only way to get the most out of meditation is to stay consistent. Make the decision to meditate everyday so you never have to wake up debating whether to meditate or not.

Meditation can be one of the most rewarding experiences of your life. If you keep at it, you will notice the difference in no time. You will realize that you are more self-aware, more mindful and just generally more at peace with life.

We live in a world where lifestyle matters, the food we eat, the clothes we wear and the way we like to spend our leisure time. But to be able to enjoy all these comforts, we need a mind which is open, happy and at rest. We might have the most spacious king-size bed with an extra-comfy mattress and simply get no sleep. We may buy tickets for the most-talked-about romantic comedy in town and sit in the hall thinking about some nasty comment from our boss instead. Our mind seems to have a mind of its own! It doesn't really stick to where we want it to be. So, what do we do?

A few minutes just for ourselves, to be still and silent in our own space. Those few minutes of stillness give deep rest to the mind and relax it. When the mind is at rest, we are better able to enjoy ourselves wherever we go, whatever we do, because we are completely in the moment.

Make meditation an integral part of your life and increase your happiness quotient generously. You can start with a few online guided meditations, for an experience, or get your own mantra to meditate. Cheers to a happy life with meditation!

Quick Tips to Include Meditation as a Lifestyle

Do it anytime, anywhere! Morning, before lunch, or evening it's your choice. At home, in office, in the garden or in a mall you are sure to find a quiet corner for just 15 minutes

You can choose to meditate alone in privacy or sit with a group of friends. Group meditation is always more effective though.

Let your mood not be a hindrance in meditation. On days you are happy, you may be all excited to meditate but when things are not so good, there is all the more reason to meditate. It can help you get over emotional highs and lows.

What is the importance of Meditation

Meditation holds profound importance for holistic well-being, impacting various aspects of physical, mental, and emotional health. The significance of meditation extends beyond spiritual practices, as scientific research continues to validate its positive effects. Here are several key reasons highlighting the importance of meditation:

1. **Stress Reduction:** One of the most well-documented benefits of meditation is its ability to reduce stress. Regular meditation practices have been shown to lower cortisol levels, the hormone associated with stress, leading to a greater sense of calm and relaxation.

2. **Enhanced Emotional Well-Being:** Meditation fosters emotional resilience and a positive outlook. It helps individuals manage and regulate emotions, reducing symptoms of anxiety and depression. The practice encourages a mindful awareness of emotions without being overwhelmed by them.
3. **Improved Concentration and Focus:** Meditation cultivates mindfulness, enhancing concentration and cognitive function. Practitioners often experience improved attention spans, better memory retention, and increased ability to focus on tasks.
4. **Better Sleep Quality:** Regular meditation has been linked to improved sleep quality. Mindfulness practices can help calm the mind, reduce racing thoughts, and alleviate insomnia, promoting a restful night's sleep.
5. **Physical Health Benefits:** Meditation contributes to physical well-being by positively impacting various bodily functions. It has been associated with lower blood pressure, improved cardiovascular health, and enhanced immune system function.
6. **Pain Management:** Chronic pain sufferers often find relief through mindfulness meditation. By cultivating a non-judgmental awareness of pain sensations, individuals can change their relationship to pain, leading to improved pain management.
7. **Mind-Body Connection:** Meditation emphasizes the connection between the mind and the body. It encourages individuals to become attuned to bodily sensations, promoting self-awareness and a deeper understanding of the mind-body relationship.
8. **Increased Self-Awareness:** Meditation facilitates self-exploration and self-discovery. Through introspection, individuals gain insights into their

thought patterns, behaviors, and motivations, fostering a greater understanding of themselves.

9. **Strengthening Resilience:** The practice of meditation cultivates resilience in the face of challenges. It teaches individuals to approach difficulties with a calm and centered mindset, reducing the impact of stressors on mental and emotional well-being.

The importance of meditation lies in its ability to promote a holistic state of well-being, touching every dimension of an individual's life. As a versatile and accessible practice, meditation offers a path to self-improvement, stress reduction, and a deeper connection to the present moment. The growing body of research supporting these benefits underscores the significance of integrating meditation into daily life for a healthier, more balanced, and fulfilling existence.

Components of Meditation

1. **Mindfulness and Awareness:** Central to meditation is the cultivation of mindfulness and awareness. This involves observing thoughts and sensations without judgment, allowing them to come and go like ripples in a tranquil pond. Through mindfulness, practitioners develop a heightened sense of presence, anchoring themselves in the richness of each moment.
2. **Breath as the Anchor:** The breath serves as a timeless anchor in meditation. Focusing on the rhythm of inhalation and exhalation grounds individuals in the present, serving as a point of concentration. This intentional breath awareness not only calms the mind but also connects the practitioner to the vital life force flowing within.
3. **Posture and Physical Awareness:** The physical aspect of meditation is embodied in posture.

Whether seated in lotus position or comfortably in a chair, the spine erects and the body relaxed, the posture reflects a harmonious balance between alertness and ease. Physical awareness extends beyond posture to the sensations within the body, fostering a connection between the mind and its earthly vessel.

4. **Guided Visualizations:** Guided visualizations are a powerful component of meditation, leading practitioners on an inward journey through the landscape of their minds. These visualizations may range from serene natural settings to symbolic imagery, unlocking the door to the subconscious and inviting a profound sense of peace and insight.
5. **Mantra Meditation:** The repetition of sacred sounds or words, known as mantra meditation, resonates as an ancient practice that transcends cultural boundaries. Mantras serve as a focal point, aligning the mind with a vibration that goes beyond linguistic meaning. This repetitive chanting not only stills the mind but also opens pathways to a deeper understanding of the self.

Mindfulness and Awareness in Meditation

1. Process of Mindfulness and Awareness:

Focus on the Present Moment: Mindfulness in meditation involves bringing full attention to the present moment. Instead of dwelling on the past or anticipating the future, practitioners aim to anchor themselves in the now.

Observation without Judgment: Awareness entails observing thoughts, feelings, and sensations without judgment. It involves a non-reactive stance, allowing experiences to come and go without attachment or aversion.

Breath as an Anchor: Often, mindfulness practices

use the breath as an anchor. Focusing on the sensations of breathing—inhaling and exhaling—helps ground the mind in the present and serves as a point of concentration.

2. Importance of Mindfulness and Awareness:

Stress Reduction: Mindfulness and awareness in meditation have a profound impact on stress reduction. By staying present and observing thoughts without getting entangled in them, individuals can break the cycle of stress.

Emotional Regulation: Cultivating mindfulness enhances emotional regulation. It allows practitioners to become more aware of their emotional states, providing the space to respond thoughtfully rather than react impulsively.

Improved Concentration: The practice of focusing on the present moment hones concentration skills. This heightened concentration often translates into improved performance in daily tasks and activities.

Enhanced Self-Awareness: Mindfulness fosters self-awareness by encouraging individuals to observe their thoughts and emotions objectively. This self-awareness forms the basis for personal growth and transformation.

3. How to Achieve Mindfulness and Awareness in Meditation:

Start with the Breath: Begin your meditation practice by paying attention to your breath. Feel the sensation of each inhalation and exhalation. This serves as a foundational anchor for mindfulness.

Body Scan Meditation: Progressively focus on different parts of your body, observing sensations without judgment. This practice enhances awareness of bodily experiences and promotes relaxation.

Guided Meditations: Utilize guided meditations that direct attention to various aspects of the present moment.

Guided sessions can be especially helpful for beginners, offering structured guidance.

Mindful Walking: Extend mindfulness beyond seated meditation by practicing mindful walking. Pay attention to each step, the sensation of movement, and the surrounding environment.

Use Mindfulness Apps: Explore mindfulness apps that offer guided meditations and mindfulness exercises. These apps often provide a structured approach, making it easier for individuals to incorporate mindfulness into their routine.

4. Incorporating Mindfulness into Daily Life:

Mindful Eating: Bring mindfulness to your meals by savoring each bite, paying attention to flavors, textures, and the act of eating. This practice enhances the connection between mind and body.

Mindful Listening: Practice active and mindful listening during conversations. Give your full attention to the speaker, without formulating responses in your mind, fostering better understanding and communication.

Mindful Breathing Breaks: Take short mindful breathing breaks throughout the day. Pause, take a few deep breaths, and center yourself in the present moment, especially during hectic or stressful periods.

Reflective Journaling: Engage in reflective journaling to enhance self-awareness. Write about your experiences, thoughts, and emotions, fostering a deeper understanding of your inner world.

5. Consistency and Patience:

Regular Practice: Consistency is key to developing mindfulness and awareness. Establish a regular meditation practice, even if it's just a few minutes each day. Over time, this consistency deepens the benefits.

Cultivate Patience: Mindfulness is a skill that develops gradually. Be patient with yourself, acknowledging that the mind may wander during meditation. Gently bring your focus back to the present without self-judgment.

Progressive Growth: As you consistently practice mindfulness and awareness, you'll notice a progressive growth in your ability to stay present, observe thoughts impartially, and navigate daily challenges with greater ease.

Mindfulness and awareness in meditation form the cornerstone of a transformative practice. By embracing the present moment with a non-judgmental awareness, individuals can unlock the myriad benefits of reduced stress, enhanced emotional well-being, improved concentration, and a deeper connection to their inner selves. Through consistent practice and a patient approach, mindfulness becomes not just a meditation technique but a way of life that enriches every aspect of one's existence.

Breath as the Anchor in Meditation

1. Process of Using Breath as the Anchor:

Find a Comfortable Posture: Begin by sitting in a comfortable and upright position. You can sit on a chair with your feet flat on the floor or cross-legged on a cushion.

Bring Attention to the Breath: Close your eyes and gently bring your attention to your breath. Notice the sensation of each inhale and exhale.

Natural Breath Observation: Allow your breath to flow naturally without attempting to control it. Observe the breath as it enters and leaves the body.

Focus on a Specific Point: Some practitioners find it helpful to focus on a specific point where they feel the breath most distinctly, such as the nostrils, chest, or abdomen.

Gentle Redirecting: If your mind starts to wander, gently redirect your focus back to the breath. Acknowledge any thoughts without judgment and return your attention to the present moment.

2. Importance of Using Breath as the Anchor:

Cultivating Present-Moment Awareness: Breath serves as a reliable anchor to the present moment. By focusing on the breath, individuals ground themselves in the here and now, fostering mindfulness.

Stress Reduction: Using the breath as the anchor has a calming effect on the nervous system. This, in turn, reduces stress and promotes a sense of relaxation and ease.

Enhanced Concentration: The rhythmic nature of the breath provides a stable focal point for the mind. Regular practice enhances concentration and helps quiet the mental chatter.

Connection to the Body: Observing the breath brings attention to the physical sensations associated with breathing, fostering a deeper connection between the mind and the body.

3. How to Achieve Using Breath as the Anchor:

Mindful Observation: Begin by mindfully observing the natural flow of your breath. Notice the sensation of the breath entering and leaving the body.

Counting Breaths: Some find it helpful to count each breath to maintain focus. Inhale, exhale—counting up to a certain number before starting over. This practice enhances concentration.

Lengthening the Breath: Experiment with lengthening the duration of your breath. Inhale slowly, hold briefly, and exhale with intention. This can deepen the sense of mindfulness.

Body Scan with Breath Awareness: Combine breath awareness with a body scan. As you inhale and exhale, progressively bring attention to different parts of your body, relaxing and releasing tension.

4. Incorporating Breath as the Anchor into Daily Life:

Mindful Breathing Breaks: Take short mindful breathing breaks throughout the day. Pause, take a few conscious breaths, and bring your attention to the present moment, especially during hectic or stressful periods.

Mindful Walking with Breath Awareness: Extend the practice to mindful walking. Coordinate your steps with your breath, paying attention to the sensation of movement and the rhythmic nature of each step.

Breath Awareness during Routine Tasks: Infuse breath awareness into routine activities. Whether washing dishes or waiting in line, bring your attention to the breath, grounding yourself in the simplicity of the present moment.

5. Consistency and Patience:

Regular Practice: Consistency is crucial when using the breath as the anchor. Establish a regular meditation practice, dedicating time each day to cultivate mindfulness through breath awareness.

Gentle Redirecting: If your mind wanders during meditation, practice gentle redirection. Acknowledge any distractions, let them go, and guide your focus back to the breath without self-judgment.

Progressive Deepening: Over time, the practice of using the breath as the anchor deepens. You may notice increased clarity, a sense of inner calm, and an enhanced ability to stay present even in challenging situations.

6. Benefits Beyond Meditation:

Stress Resilience: Regularly using the breath as the anchor builds stress resilience, allowing individuals to respond to challenges with greater equanimity.

Improved Sleep: Practicing breath awareness before bedtime can contribute to improved sleep quality, as it helps calm the mind and prepare the body for relaxation.

Emotional Regulation: Breath awareness supports emotional regulation, providing a tool for responding thoughtfully to emotions rather than reacting impulsively.

Increased Mindfulness in Daily Life: The benefits of using the breath as the anchor extend beyond meditation, leading to increased mindfulness and presence in various aspects of daily life.

Using breath as the anchor in meditation is a powerful practice with far-reaching benefits. It serves as a gateway to present-moment awareness, stress reduction, enhanced concentration, and a deeper connection to the self. Through consistent and patient practice, individuals can integrate this simple yet profound technique into their daily lives, fostering a sense of calm, clarity, and mindfulness.

Posture and Physical Awareness in Meditation

1. Process of Establishing Posture and Physical Awareness:

Sit Comfortably: Find a comfortable seated position. You can sit on a chair with your feet flat on the floor or cross-legged on a cushion. The key is to maintain a position that allows you to be alert and at ease.

Erect Spine: Straighten your spine without being rigid. Imagine a string pulling you upward from the top of your head, creating a natural alignment. This promotes both alertness and relaxation.

Relaxed Shoulders: Allow your shoulders to relax and drop naturally. Tension in the shoulders can hinder the flow of energy, so consciously release any tightness.

Hands and Arms: Rest your hands on your lap, with

palms facing upward or downward. Alternatively, you can adopt a specific hand mudra. Keep your arms relaxed, with elbows slightly away from your body.

Neck and Head Alignment: Align your head with your spine, neither tilted forward nor backward. Let your chin be slightly tucked in. This alignment supports a clear and focused mind.

Closed or Open Eyes: Depending on your preference or the meditation technique, you can close your eyes or keep them open with a soft gaze, maintaining a gentle focus on a point in front of you.

2. Importance of Posture and Physical Awareness

Supports Mental Alertness: A proper meditation posture supports mental alertness and prevents drowsiness. The erect spine and open chest contribute to a state of wakeful presence.

Facilitates Energy Flow: A balanced posture helps facilitate the flow of energy throughout the body. When the body is aligned, energy can move freely, contributing to a sense of vitality.

Reduces Physical Discomfort: Maintaining a comfortable posture reduces the likelihood of physical discomfort during meditation. This allows practitioners to focus their attention inward without distraction.

Enhances Mind-Body Connection: Conscious awareness of the body during meditation fosters a deeper mind-body connection. This awareness can lead to a greater understanding of how the body responds to thoughts and emotions.

3. How to Achieve Posture and Physical Awareness

Body Scan Meditation: Begin your meditation by conducting a body scan. Bring your awareness to each part of your body, starting from your toes and moving upward. Notice areas of tension and consciously release them.

Mindful Movement: Before settling into meditation, engage in mindful movement or stretching. This can help release any physical tension and bring your attention to the sensations in your body.

Regular Check-ins: During meditation, periodically check in with your body. Notice if there's any tension or discomfort, and adjust your posture accordingly. Regular check-ins enhance overall comfort.

Yoga or Stretching Practices: Incorporate yoga or stretching practices into your routine to promote flexibility and body awareness. These practices can complement your meditation by preparing the body for stillness.

4. Incorporating Posture and Physical Awareness into Daily Life

Mindful Sitting: Practice mindful sitting throughout the day. Whether at your desk, in a meeting, or during meals, pay attention to your posture. Sit upright, supporting a sense of presence and attentiveness.

Conscious Walking: Bring awareness to your posture while walking. Maintain an upright stance, and be mindful of each step. Walking with awareness can be a moving meditation, promoting a sense of grounding.

Ergonomics at Work: If you have a desk job, ensure your workspace is ergonomically friendly. Adjust your chair and computer height to support good posture, reducing physical strain.

5. Consistency and Patience

Regular Practice: Consistency is essential for developing a mindful posture. Regularly practice maintaining an alert and comfortable posture during meditation sessions.

Gradual Progress: If you are new to meditation or adjusting your posture, progress gradually. Allow your body to adapt to the changes, and be patient with the process.

Mindful Corrections: During meditation, make mindful corrections to your posture as needed. This can be done without disrupting the flow of your practice, ensuring that you maintain a comfortable position.

6. Benefits Beyond Meditation

Improved Posture in Daily Life: Conscious attention to posture during meditation can translate into improved posture in daily life. This, in turn, contributes to overall physical well-being.

Reduced Physical Tension: Regularly practicing awareness of physical sensations can reduce chronic tension. As you become more attuned to your body, you can release tension more effectively.

Enhanced Body Awareness: Posture and physical awareness in meditation contribute to a heightened sense of body awareness. This awareness extends beyond meditation, promoting a mindful and embodied presence.

Posture and physical awareness play a vital role in meditation, fostering a conducive environment for inner stillness and mindfulness. By adopting a comfortable and alert posture, practitioners not only support their meditation practice but also cultivate a deeper connection between mind and body. Through consistent awareness and gentle adjustments, individuals can integrate mindful posture into their daily lives, promoting physical comfort, mental alertness, and overall well-being.

Guided Visualizations in Meditation

Process of Guided Visualizations

The guided visualization typically starts setting an intention for the practice or creating a mental space for relaxation and openness.

Preparation: Find a quiet and comfortable space for your meditation practice. Sit or lie down in a relaxed position, ensuring you won't be disturbed. Close your eyes to enhance your focus on the guided visualization.

Engaging the Senses: The guide invites participants to engage their senses by describing a scene or scenario in vivid detail. This may include visual elements, sounds, textures, and even scents, creating a multisensory experience.

Immersive Storytelling: The guide leads participants through a narrative, encouraging them to mentally participate in the described scenario. This storytelling may involve a journey, a peaceful scene, or a symbolic experience.

Reflective Prompts: At various points, the guide may introduce reflective prompts to deepen the experience. This could involve exploring emotions, gaining insights, or connecting with specific aspects of the visualization.

The guided visualization concludes by gently bringing participants back to the present moment. The guide may encourage a gradual return to awareness, thanking participants for their presence in the visualization.

2. Importance of Guided Visualizations

Stress Reduction and Relaxation: Guided visualizations are effective for reducing stress and inducing a state of relaxation. The immersive experience takes participants away from daily worries, promoting mental calmness.

Enhanced Creativity: Engaging the imagination in guided visualizations stimulates creativity. Participants can explore new ideas, perspectives, and possibilities, fostering a sense of innovation and inspiration.

Emotional Healing: Guided visualizations can be a powerful tool for emotional healing. Exploring emotions within the safe space of visualization allows for processing and releasing pent-up feelings.

Increased Mindfulness: Through the focused attention required in visualizations, participants cultivate mindfulness. The practice encourages being fully present in the unfolding mental landscape, honing the skill of sustained attention.

3. Process of Guided Visualizations

Find a Suitable Guide: Utilize guided meditation resources from experienced guides. This could involve attending guided meditation sessions, using meditation apps, or accessing online platforms offering guided visualizations.

Create a Comfortable Space: Ensure you are in a comfortable and quiet space where you can fully immerse yourself in the guided visualization without distractions.

Open Mind and Imagination: Approach guided visualizations with an open mind and a willingness to engage your imagination. Let go of any preconceived notions and allow the experience to unfold organically.

Deep Breathing: Begin the session with a few deep breaths to relax your body and mind. Deep breathing can help create a receptive state for the visualization journey.

4. Incorporating Guided Visualizations into Daily Life

Short Breaks: Use guided visualizations during short breaks in your day. Taking a few minutes to engage in a visualization can refresh your mind and provide a mental reset.

Morning or Evening Ritual: Make guided visualizations a part of your morning or evening ritual. This can set a positive tone for the day ahead or help unwind and relax before bedtime.

Creativity Boost: If you're working on a creative project, incorporate guided visualizations to spark new ideas and perspectives. It can break through mental blocks and unleash creative energy.

5. Consistency and Patience

Regular Practice: Consistency is key when integrating guided visualizations into your routine. Aim for regular practice to experience the cumulative benefits over time.

Patient Exploration: Allow the experience to unfold without expectations. Guided visualizations are a form of exploration, and each session may offer different insights and sensations.

Adapt to Preferences: Explore different guides and styles of guided visualizations to find what resonates best with you. Not every visualization will be equally effective, so adapt based on your preferences and experiences.

6. Benefits Beyond Meditation

Improved Focus: Regular practice of guided visualizations can enhance overall focus and concentration. The sharpening of mental imagery can spill over into daily tasks and activities.

Enhanced Problem-Solving: Engaging in creative visualizations can stimulate problem-solving skills. It encourages thinking outside the box and exploring novel solutions to challenges.

Mind-Body Connection: Guided visualizations foster a stronger connection between the mind and body. By vividly imagining sensations and experiences, participants deepen their awareness of the mind-body relationship.

In summary, guided visualizations in meditation offer a dynamic and imaginative approach to mindfulness. They serve as a gateway to relaxation, creativity, and emotional exploration. By incorporating guided visualizations into your routine with consistency and an open mind, you can tap into their transformative potential for enhanced well-being and self-discovery.

Mantra Meditation in Meditation

1. Process of Mantra Meditation

Choose a Mantra: Select a mantra that holds personal significance or one traditionally used in mantra meditation. Common mantras include "Om," "So Hum," or a word that resonates with your intention or spiritual practice.

Find a Comfortable Posture: Sit in a comfortable position with an upright spine. You can sit on a cushion or chair with your hands resting on your lap. Close your eyes to turn your focus inward.

Focus on the Breath Initially: Begin by taking a few deep breaths to center yourself. Allow your breath to become natural, and focus on the sensation of each inhalation and exhalation for a few moments.

Introduce the Mantra: Start repeating the chosen mantra silently in your mind. You can synchronize the mantra with your breath, reciting it mentally on each inhale and exhale. Alternatively, you may repeat the mantra at your own pace.

Maintain Gentle Focus: As you repeat the mantra, gently bring your attention back to it whenever your mind starts to wander. The mantra becomes a point of focus, helping to quiet mental chatter and distractions.

Let Go of Effort: Allow the repetition of the mantra to become effortless. Release any attachment to specific outcomes or experiences. Let the mantra flow naturally, becoming a subtle backdrop to your meditation.

Periods of Silence: Introduce periods of silence between repetitions of the mantra. Allow yourself to rest in the stillness and observe any residual vibrations or sensations.

2. Importance of Mantra Meditation

Concentration and Focus: Mantra meditation enhances concentration and focus by providing a focal point for the mind. The rhythmic repetition of the mantra helps anchor the mind in the present moment.

Inner Calm and Relaxation: The rhythmic chanting of a mantra induces a state of inner calm and relaxation. It has a soothing effect on the nervous system, promoting a sense of peace and tranquility.

Spiritual Connection: Many practitioners use mantra meditation as a tool for spiritual connection. The repetitive chanting creates a meditative space for introspection, self-discovery, and connection with higher states of consciousness.

Sound and Vibration: The sound and vibration of the mantra are believed to have a transformative effect on the mind and body. This resonant quality contributes to the overall meditative experience.

3. Process of Mantra Meditation

Choose a Meaningful Mantra: Select a mantra that holds personal significance or aligns with your spiritual or meditative goals. Experiment with different mantras to find one that resonates with you.

Start Slowly: If you're new to mantra meditation, start slowly with short sessions. Begin with a few minutes and gradually extend the duration as you become more comfortable with the practice.

Use Mala Beads: Mala beads, consisting of 108 beads, can be used to count repetitions of the mantra. Each bead represents a repetition, allowing you to maintain focus and track your progress.

Integrate Breath Awareness: Combine mantra meditation with breath awareness. Synchronize the repetition of the mantra with your breath, creating a harmonious rhythm that deepens the meditative experience.

4. Incorporating Mantra Meditation into Daily Life

Morning Routine: Include mantra meditation in your morning routine. It can set a positive tone for the day and create a centered and focused mindset.

Stressful Moments: Turn to mantra meditation during moments of stress or overwhelm. The practice can serve as a quick and effective tool for calming the mind in challenging situations.

Before Sleep: Practice mantra meditation before bedtime to relax the mind and promote restful sleep. This can help release tension accumulated throughout the day.

5. Consistency and Patience

Regular Practice: Consistency is essential in mantra meditation. Establish a regular practice schedule, whether daily or a few times a week, to experience the cumulative benefits over time.

Patient Approach: Approach mantra meditation with patience. The benefits may unfold gradually, and the practice may evolve over time. Allow yourself the space to explore and grow within the practice.

6. Benefits Beyond Meditation

Stress Reduction: Mantra meditation is a powerful tool for stress reduction. The rhythmic repetition of the mantra induces a state of relaxation, helping to alleviate stress and tension.

Enhanced Mindfulness: The focused nature of mantra meditation cultivates mindfulness. It trains the mind to stay present, fostering a heightened awareness of thoughts, emotions, and the surrounding environment.

Clarity of Mind: Regular practice of mantra meditation

can lead to a clearer and calmer mind. It promotes mental clarity, enabling practitioners to approach challenges with a centered and focused mindset.

Spiritual Growth: For those on a spiritual journey, mantra meditation can be a vehicle for spiritual growth. The practice creates a sacred space for inner exploration and connection with higher states of consciousness.

Mantra meditation is a profound and accessible practice with diverse benefits for the mind, body, and spirit. By incorporating mantra meditation into your routine with consistency and an open heart, you can tap into its transformative power and cultivate a sense of inner peace, focus, and spiritual connection.

Beyond the Cushion - Integrating Meditation into Daily Life

Meditation is not confined to the moments spent in stillness; its essence extends into the tapestry of everyday life. The cultivation of mindfulness can be seamlessly woven into daily activities, transforming routine tasks into opportunities for presence and awareness. Whether sipping a cup of tea, walking in nature, or engaging in mundane chores, the principles of meditation infuse each moment with a sacred quality, inviting individuals to live more consciously.

Integrating meditation into your daily life involves making mindfulness a natural and seamless part of your routine.

Here are practical steps to help incorporate meditation into everyday activities:

1. **Start with Realistic Goals:** Begin with realistic expectations. If you're new to meditation, start with short sessions, such as 5-10 minutes, and gradually extend the duration as you become more comfortable.

2. **Establish a Routine:** Set a specific time each day for meditation. Whether it's in the morning, during lunch, or before bedtime, having a consistent schedule helps build a habit.
3. **Create a Dedicated Space:** Designate a quiet and comfortable space for meditation. It could be a corner of a room, a cushion in a quiet area, or even a comfortable chair. Having a dedicated space signals to your mind that it's time for introspection.
4. **Incorporate Mindful Moments:** Infuse mindfulness into daily activities. Pay full attention to the present moment while walking, eating, or doing routine tasks. This can serve as a form of "informal" meditation.
5. **Use Meditation Apps:** Leverage meditation apps that offer guided sessions. These apps often provide flexibility in terms of session duration and focus areas, making it easier to integrate meditation into a busy schedule.
6. **Mindful Breathing Breaks:** Take short breaks during the day for mindful breathing. Pause, take a few deep breaths, and center yourself in the present moment. This practice can be especially beneficial during stressful moments.
7. **Connect Meditation to Existing Habits:** Link meditation to existing habits. For example, meditate right after brushing your teeth or tie it to your morning coffee routine. Associating meditation with established habits helps it become a natural part of your day.
8. **Explore Various Meditation Techniques:** Experiment with different meditation techniques. Whether it's mindfulness, mantra meditation, or loving-kindness meditation, find an approach that

resonates with you and fits into your lifestyle.

9. **Mindful Technology Use:** Use technology mindfully. Instead of mindlessly scrolling through your phone, consider using mindfulness apps or guided meditations during screen time breaks.
10. **Lunchtime Meditation:** Utilize lunch breaks for meditation. Find a quiet space, set a timer, and use a guided meditation app if needed. This can help you recharge for the afternoon.
11. **Evening Wind-Down:** Incorporate meditation into your evening wind-down routine. A calming meditation before bedtime can prepare your mind for a restful sleep.
12. **Group Meditation Sessions:** Join group meditation sessions, either in-person or virtually. Group meditation can provide accountability and a sense of community, making it more likely for you to stick to your practice.
13. **Mindful Walking:** Practice mindful walking. Instead of rushing from one place to another, slow down and pay attention to each step. This can be a simple yet effective way to integrate mindfulness into your daily movements.
14. **Reflective Journaling:** Combine meditation with reflective journaling. After a meditation session, take a few moments to jot down any thoughts, insights, or feelings that arose during the practice.
15. **Be Kind to Yourself:** Embrace imperfection and be kind to yourself. If you miss a session or find it challenging at times, acknowledge it without judgment. Cultivating a compassionate attitude towards yourself supports sustainable meditation practice.

By incorporating these steps into your daily life, you'll gradually integrate meditation into your routine, making it a natural and beneficial part of your overall well-being.

The Journey Continues

As we navigate the realms of meditation, it becomes evident that this ancient practice is not a destination but a perpetual journey. The importance lies not only in the stillness found within the moments of meditation but in the subtle transformation that permeates every facet of existence. With mindfulness as our guide and breath as our anchor, the journey of meditation unfolds, revealing the boundless expanses of self-discovery, inner peace, and interconnectedness. In the chapters that follow, we will explore specific meditation techniques, delve into the science behind its profound effects, and offer practical guidance for integrating this transformative practice into our lives. The journey continues, and with each breath, we step into the profound and timeless realm of meditation.

13

Money Matters

"It's not the money that matters, it's how you use it that determines it's value."

Knowledge of money and handling of finance is very important. We are striving hard each day to earn money, if we are unaware of how to handle, save and put our money to the right use it is never going to increase and we will always be stuck in the process of earning money. Since I was always intrigued about saving and banking was my career choice hence naturally, I was drawn towards finding out how to grow money on its own and the term achieving "Financial freedom" became my next target.

The thought that I have to have the freedom to live life as I want with the freedom to choose where to live, what to do, travel etc. were included in this decision making. I started from nothing, reached a very important position and did pretty much very good there till I decided to give it up; reason I was not satisfied with what I was doing!! Starting again was tougher as I did not know where to start in the beginning, me being an organized processor, I collected all the data and stock of what I had, what I needed to live than what I wanted to achieve. For me identifying these step by step provided clarity and from there I started to focus on creating. The difference this time was I was clearer on my 'why' and 'where to'. Goals were clear slowly; here I would like to remind you that this clarity is not a one-step product, like meditation grows on you so does your goals and purpose. More the time we spent in retrospection the better.

Key concepts and principles of personal finance

Here's an overview of key concepts and principles focusing on these helped me:

1. **Budgeting:** Creating a plan for how you will spend and save your money. Helps manage expenses, save for goals, and avoid debt.
2. **Saving and Investing:** Setting aside money for future needs or emergencies. Putting money into assets with the expectation of generating a return. Allows your money to grow over time and build wealth.
3. **Emergency Fund:** A savings fund set aside for unexpected expenses or emergencies. Provides a financial safety net and reduces the need for debt in emergencies.
4. **Credit and Debt Management:** A numerical representation of creditworthiness. Effectively

handling and repaying debts affects loan approval, interest rates, and overall financial health.

5. **Insurance:** Insurance are of different types Life, health, auto, home, and more. Protects against financial loss due to unexpected events.
6. **Retirement Planning:** Saving and investing for retirement. Ensures financial security during retirement years.
7. **Tax Planning:** Strategizing to minimize tax liabilities. Maximizes after-tax income and wealth.
8. **Financial Goals:** Short-term (e.g., vacation), medium-term (e.g., buying a home), and long-term (e.g., retirement). Guides financial decisions and priorities.

Some basics on Investment

1. Types of Investments

There are various types of investments, each with its own characteristics, risk profiles, and potential returns. Here are some common types of investments:

Stocks: Investors buy shares of a company, making them partial owners. Stock values can fluctuate based on the company's performance and market conditions.

Bonds: Investors lend money to a government or corporation in exchange for periodic interest payments and the return of the principal amount at maturity.

Mutual Funds: Pooled funds from multiple investors are managed by a professional fund manager who invests in a diversified portfolio of stocks, bonds, or other securities.

Exchange-Traded Funds (ETFs): Similar to mutual funds, ETFs are investment funds traded on stock exchanges. They often track an index or a commodity and are traded like a stock.

Real Estate: Investment in physical properties, such as residential or commercial real estate, with the potential for rental income and property value appreciation.

Cryptocurrencies: Digital or virtual currencies that use cryptography for security. Bitcoin, Ethereum, and other cryptocurrencies are examples.

Certificates of Deposit (CDs): Time deposits offered by banks with a fixed interest rate and maturity date. They are considered low-risk but offer lower returns compared to riskier investments.

Options: Financial derivatives that give investors the right, but not the obligation, to buy or sell an asset at a predetermined price within a specified time frame.

Commodities: Physical goods like gold, silver, oil, or agricultural products that can be traded on commodity exchanges.

Precious Metals: Investments in precious metals like gold, silver, platinum, and palladium, often used as a hedge against inflation and economic uncertainty.

Savings Accounts: Low-risk, interest-bearing accounts offered by banks, providing a safe place to store money with minimal returns.

Retirement Accounts: Tax-advantaged accounts designed for long-term retirement savings, often including a mix of stocks, bonds, and mutual funds.

Hedge Funds: Investment funds managed by professional portfolio managers, often employing advanced strategies and open to accredited investors.

Investors often create portfolios that include a mix of these investment types to diversify and manage risk. The choice of investments depends on factors such as financial goals, risk tolerance, and time horizon. It's essential to conduct thorough research or seek advice from financial professionals before making investment decisions.

2. Risk and Return

The relationship between risk and return is a fundamental concept in finance. Generally, the idea is that higher potential returns are associated with higher levels of risk. Here's a breakdown of the risk-return relationship:

Low-Risk, Low-Return Investments:

Savings Accounts and CDs: These are considered low-risk investments. They offer capital preservation and guaranteed returns, but the trade-off is that the returns are relatively low.

Moderate-Risk, Moderate-Return Investments:

Bonds: While bonds are generally less risky than stocks, they still carry some risk, especially if interest rates rise. The returns are usually higher than those from savings accounts or CDs.

Blue-Chip Stocks: Large, well-established companies with a history of stable performance often provide moderate returns with moderate risk.

Diversified Mutual Funds: Mutual funds that invest in a mix of stocks and bonds can provide a balanced risk-return profile.

High-Risk, High-Return Investments:

Small-Cap Stocks: Smaller companies may have higher growth potential but also come with higher volatility and risk.

Options and Derivatives: These financial instruments can offer significant returns but involve a higher level of complexity and risk.

Cryptocurrencies: While some investors have seen substantial returns, the cryptocurrency market is highly volatile, making it a high-risk, high-return investment.

Venture Capital and Startups: Investing in new, unproven businesses can yield high returns, but the risk of failure is also significant.

High-Yield (Junk) Bonds: Bonds issued by less creditworthy companies may offer higher returns, but they come with a higher risk of default.

It's crucial for investors to understand their risk tolerance, financial goals, and investment horizon. Diversification, the practice of spreading investments across different asset classes, can help manage risk. While seeking higher returns is often desirable, it's important to carefully consider the associated risks and conduct thorough research or seek advice before making investment decisions.

Investors should also be aware of the distinction between systematic risk (market-wide risk that cannot be eliminated through diversification) and unsystematic risk (specific to a particular asset and can be mitigated through diversification). Balancing these types of risks is key to constructing a well-rounded investment portfolio.

3. Diversification

Diversification is a risk management strategy that involves spreading investments across different assets or asset classes to reduce the impact of the poor performance of a single investment on the overall portfolio. The goal is to achieve a balance between risk and return. Here are key aspects of diversification in investment:

Geographic Diversification: Invest in assets from different regions or countries to reduce the impact of economic or geopolitical events specific to one location.

Industry Sectors: Within the stock market, diversify across different industries to reduce the risk associated with sector-specific challenges.

Investment Styles: Diversify between growth and

value investments to balance exposure to different market conditions.

Investment Vehicles: Utilize a mix of investment vehicles, such as stocks, bonds, mutual funds, exchange-traded funds (ETFs), and other instruments, to achieve a well-rounded portfolio.

Currency Diversification: If investing internationally, consider the impact of currency fluctuations and diversify across currencies to mitigate currency risk.

Risk Tolerance and Time Horizon: Align the diversification strategy with your risk tolerance and investment time horizon. Younger investors with a longer time horizon may have a higher risk tolerance and can afford to take on more aggressive, potentially higher-returning investments.

Regular Rebalancing: Periodically review and rebalance your portfolio to ensure that the asset allocation remains in line with your investment goals. Market movements can cause the original allocation to shift over time.

Avoid Overconcentration: Avoid overconcentration in a single stock or a small number of assets. This reduces the risk of a significant loss if one investment performs poorly.

Consider Alternatives: Explore alternative investments, such as commodities, precious metals, or private equity, to add further diversification.

Diversification does not eliminate risk entirely, but it can help manage and mitigate risks associated with individual investments. It is essential to conduct thorough research, understand the characteristics of each investment, and regularly reassess your portfolio's diversification strategy based on your financial goals and market conditions. Diversification is a dynamic process that should evolve over time as your financial situation changes and as market conditions shift.

4. Compounding

Compounding is a powerful concept in investing that refers to the ability of an investment to generate earnings, which are then reinvested to generate additional earnings in subsequent periods. Over time, compounding can lead to significant growth in the value of an investment. The key to compounding is that earnings from an investment not only come from the initial principal but also from the reinvestment of those earnings.

Here are key points to understand about compounding in investment

Compound Interest: In the context of interest-bearing investments, such as savings accounts, bonds, or certain types of loans, compound interest refers to the interest calculated not only on the initial principal but also on the accumulated interest from previous periods.

Reinvestment of Earnings: In investments like stocks or funds, earnings in the form of dividends or capital gains are often automatically reinvested, leading to an increase in the investment's overall value.

Time Horizon: The longer the time an investment is allowed to compound, the more significant its impact. Time is a crucial factor in compounding because it allows earnings to generate additional earnings over multiple periods.

Compounding Frequency: The frequency with which compounding occurs affects the overall growth. Investments that compound more frequently (daily or monthly, for example) will generally grow faster than those with less frequent compounding.

Power of Compounding: Compounding has been often referred to as the "eighth wonder of the world" and is attributed to Albert Einstein. The idea is that compounding can turn a relatively small amount of money into a substantial sum over an extended period.

Effect on Returns: Compounding magnifies the impact of returns. For example, a 10% annual return compounded over several years can lead to a much larger total return compared to a simple linear calculation of 10% each year.

Importance of Consistency: Consistent and disciplined contributions or investments, along with reinvesting earnings, are key to maximizing the benefits of compounding. Regular contributions, even if small, can have a significant impact over time.

Risk and Volatility: While compounding can work to an investor's advantage, it's important to note that it can also be affected by market downturns. Volatility and losses can impede the compounding process, especially if there are withdrawals during market downturns.

Start Early: The earlier an investor starts, the more time the investment has to compound. Starting early allows for a more gradual and less aggressive approach to investing.

Compounding underscores the importance of a long-term perspective in investing and highlights the benefits of patience and consistency. It's a fundamental principle that investors can use to build wealth over time. The compounding effect becomes more pronounced as the investment horizon extends, making it a valuable tool for long-term financial planning.

5. Asset Allocation

Asset allocation is a crucial strategy in investment management that involves distributing an investment portfolio across various asset classes to achieve a balance between risk and return. The goal of asset allocation is to optimize the portfolio's performance based on an investor's financial goals, risk tolerance, and time horizon. Here are key aspects of asset allocation:

Asset Classes:

Equities (Stocks): Represent ownership in companies. Equities have the potential for high returns but come with higher volatility.

Fixed-Income (Bonds): Involve lending money to governments or corporations in exchange for periodic interest payments and the return of principal. Bonds are generally considered a lower risk than stocks.

Cash and Cash Equivalents: Include instruments like money market funds and short-term certificates of deposit. These are low-risk, highly liquid assets.

Risk Tolerance: Investors should align their asset allocation with their risk tolerance, which is their ability and willingness to withstand fluctuations in the value of their portfolio. Risk tolerance is influenced by factors such as age, financial goals, and investment experience.

Investment Goals: Asset allocation should be tailored to an investor's specific financial goals. For example, a retiree might prioritize income and capital preservation, while a young investor may focus on long-term capital appreciation.

Time Horizon: The length of time an investor plans to hold investments is a critical factor in asset allocation. Longer time horizons may allow for a more aggressive allocation, including a higher proportion of equities.

Rebalancing: Over time, market movements can cause the original asset allocation to deviate from the intended mix. Regularly rebalancing the portfolio involves adjusting the allocations to maintain the desired balance. This ensures that the portfolio remains aligned with the investor's goals and risk tolerance.

Professional Advice: Seeking advice from financial professionals, such as financial advisors or investment managers, can help investors tailor their asset allocation to their specific circumstances and goals.

Asset allocation is a dynamic process that should evolve as an investor's financial situation changes. It plays a significant role in determining portfolio performance and risk, making it an essential aspect of investment planning. Investors should regularly review their asset allocation strategy and make adjustments as needed based on changing circumstances and market conditions.

6. Market Trends

Market trends in investment refer to the general direction in which financial markets are moving over a certain period. Analyzing market trends is crucial for investors, as it helps them make informed decisions about buying, selling, or holding investments. Here are some key concepts related to market trends:

Bullish Trend: A bullish trend is characterized by rising prices and positive investor sentiment. Investors are optimistic about the market's future, leading to an increase in buying activity.

Bearish Trend: A bearish trend is characterized by falling prices and negative investor sentiment. Investors are pessimistic about the market's future, leading to an increase in selling activity.

Understanding these concepts empowers individuals to make informed financial decisions and entrepreneurs to build financially sound businesses. Continuous learning and staying updated on financial trends contribute to better financial management and long-term success.

Importance of financial knowledge for women

Financial knowledge is crucial for everyone, regardless of gender, but there are specific reasons why it is particularly important for women. Here are some key reasons highlighting the importance of financial knowledge for women:

1. **Financial Independence:** Financial knowledge empowers women to make informed decisions about their money, leading to greater financial independence. It allows women to control their financial destinies and reduce dependence on others.
2. **Career Transitions:** Women may face career interruptions due to life events like childbirth, caregiving, or other personal reasons. Financial literacy helps navigate these transitions, plan for potential income gaps, and make informed decisions about career choices.
3. **Investing for the Future:** Women generally live longer than men, and understanding how to invest for the long term is crucial for financial security in retirement. Knowledge about investment options, risk management, and compounding helps women build wealth over time.
4. **Navigating Life Changes:** Women often experience significant life changes, such as divorce or the death of a spouse. Financial literacy equips women to handle these changes, manage assets, and secure their financial well-being.
5. **Entrepreneurship:** The number of women entrepreneurs is rising globally. Financial knowledge is essential for successfully starting and managing a business, including budgeting, financial planning, and securing funding.
6. **Equal Pay and Negotiation:** Women, on average, still earn less than men in many workplaces. Financial literacy aids in negotiating salaries, understanding benefits, and advocating for fair compensation.

7. **Debt Management:** Understanding how to manage and avoid debt is crucial for financial stability. Financial knowledge helps women make sound borrowing decisions and develop strategies for debt repayment.
8. **Retirement Planning:** Women may have different retirement needs than men due to longer life expectancy and potential healthcare costs. Financial literacy enables effective retirement planning, including understanding pension options, Social Security, and individual retirement accounts.
9. **Supporting Family Finances:** Many women play a significant role in managing family finances. Financial knowledge allows women to contribute effectively to family financial decisions, budgeting, and long-term planning.
10. **Educational Planning for Children:** Financial literacy helps women plan and save for their children's education. It enables informed decisions about college savings accounts, investment strategies, and financial aid options.

Empowering women with financial knowledge, is not just about individual well-being; it contributes to the economic growth and stability of families, communities, and societies as a whole. It enables women to actively participate in economic decision-making, fostering a more inclusive and equitable financial landscape.

How women can achieve financial freedom

Achieving financial freedom is a significant goal that involves careful planning, disciplined financial habits, and strategic decision-making. Here are practical steps that women can take to work toward financial freedom:

1. Set Clear Financial Goals

2. Create a Budget
3. Build an Emergency Fund
4. Eliminate High-Interest Debt
5. Invest Wisely
6. Diversify Investments
7. Educate Yourself
8. Negotiate Salaries and Benefits
9. Create Passive Income
10. Protect Your Assets
11. Plan for Major Expenses
12. Continuously Review and Adjust
13. Cultivate a Healthy Relationship with Money
14. Plan for Long-Term Care

Achieving financial freedom is a dynamic and ongoing process. It requires dedication, strategic planning, and a commitment to continuous learning. By taking proactive steps and staying focused on long-term goals, women can work towards financial freedom and create a secure and fulfilling future.

Financial knowledge helping women to restart life

Having strong financial knowledge can be a powerful asset for women who are on a break and looking to restart their lives. Here's how a solid understanding of finances can aid in this journey, along with practical ways for women to achieve financial knowledge:

Budgeting for Transition: Understanding how to create and manage a budget helps women allocate resources effectively during a transition period. It allows for careful planning of expenses, savings, and investment for future goals.

Financial Independence: Financial literacy empowers women to take control of their financial destinies. It reduces dependency on external sources and provides the confidence to make sound financial decisions independently.

Career Decisions: Financial knowledge helps in evaluating career options and making decisions that align with long-term financial goals. It assists in negotiating salaries, understanding benefits, and planning for career growth.

Investing for the Future: Knowing how to invest wisely is crucial for building wealth over time. Women can leverage their financial knowledge to make informed investment decisions, ensuring their money works for them in the long run.

Debt Management: Understanding debt, its implications, and strategies for managing it is essential. Financial literacy enables women to make informed choices about borrowing, avoid unnecessary debt, and develop plans for debt repayment.

Entrepreneurial Ventures: For women considering entrepreneurship, financial knowledge is key to successfully starting and managing a business. It includes budgeting, financial planning, and securing funding from various sources.

Life Transitions: Women often experience significant life changes such as marriage, divorce, or becoming a caregiver. Financial literacy helps in navigating these transitions, making informed decisions, and securing financial well-being.

Retirement Planning: Planning for retirement is critical for long-term financial security. Financial knowledge assists women in understanding retirement options, creating effective retirement plans, and ensuring a comfortable lifestyle in later years.

Some Practical Ways for Women to Achieve Financial Knowledge:

Educational Resources: Utilize online courses, workshops, and educational websites focused on personal finance and investment. Many platforms offer free or affordable courses.

Books and Reading Materials: Read books on personal finance, investing, and entrepreneurship. Look for resources that cater to different levels of financial literacy.

Financial Workshops and Seminars: Attend local or virtual financial workshops and seminars. These events often cover a range of topics and provide opportunities to interact with experts.

Financial Planning Services: Consult with financial planners or advisors for personalized guidance. They can help create tailored financial plans based on individual goals and circumstances.

Networking and Mentorship: Connect with individuals who have expertise in finance or entrepreneurship. Seek mentorship from experienced professionals who can provide valuable insights and guidance.

Online Forums and Communities: Join online forums and communities where financial topics are discussed. Engage in conversations, ask questions, and learn from the experiences of others.

Podcasts and Webinars: Listen to podcasts and attend webinars that focus on financial literacy. Many experts share valuable insights through these mediums.

Financial Apps and Tools: Use financial apps and tools that simplify budgeting, tracking expenses, and managing investments. These tools often provide practical insights into personal financial management.

Continual Learning: Stay curious and committed to continual learning. The financial landscape evolves, and ongoing education ensures that women stay informed about new trends and strategies.

Community College or Adult Education Courses: Consider taking courses at local community colleges or adult education centers. Some institutions offer classes specifically designed for improving financial literacy.

Financial Blogs: Follow reputable financial blogs that cover a variety of topics, including budgeting, investing, and career planning. Many bloggers share personal stories and practical advice.

Government and Nonprofit Resources: Explore resources provided by government agencies and nonprofit organizations. These entities often offer educational materials and workshops on financial literacy.

Remember that building financial knowledge is a gradual process, and it's okay to start with the basics. Consistency and a commitment to ongoing learning are key to developing a strong foundation in financial literacy. By taking proactive steps to enhance financial knowledge, women can equip themselves with the tools needed to navigate transitions and restart their lives with confidence.

The S.A.V.E.R.S Routine

"Your entire life changes the day that you decide you will no longer accept mediocrity for yourself." **- Hal Elrod**

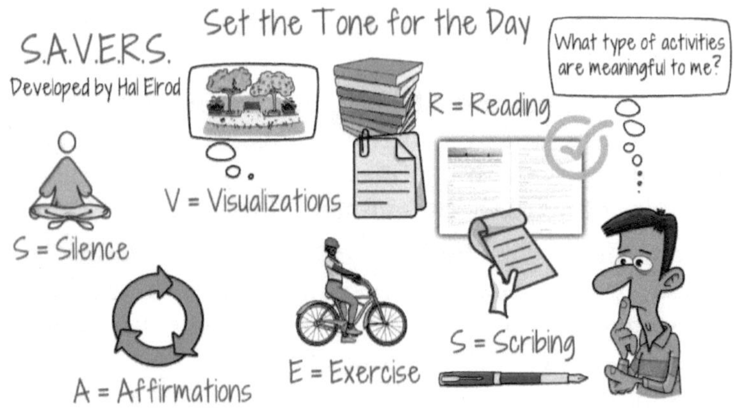

S.A.V.E.R.S in my life was introduced by my coach and it turned out to be a Powerful Plan for taking full control of life and navigating it to desired direction I wanted my life to go. I still follow it by tweaking it as it fits my routine.

The **S.A.V.E.R.S** Morning Routine for Personal Transformation is very helpful in the quest for personal development and transformative growth, the implementation of a structured morning routine can be a game-changer. Enter the **S.A.V.E.R.S**, a powerful acronym that captures a holistic approach to kickstarting your day with intention and mindfulness. Each letter represents a key practice, and collectively they form a routine that has gained popularity for its potential to enhance various aspects of life.

1. S - Silence (Meditation)

The journey of the S.A.V.E.R.S begins with the tranquil embrace of silence. Before the demands of the day unfold, allocating time for meditation allows for a stilling of the mind. Engaging in mindful breathing or a guided meditation session creates a mental sanctuary, fostering clarity and calmness. Silence becomes the foundation upon which the other practices can flourish.

Cultivating Silence as a routine

In meditation, silence is not merely the absence of sound; it is a profound state of inner stillness and tranquility. The effectiveness of silence in meditation lies in its ability to create a space where the mind can settle, distractions dissipate, and a deep connection with the present moment is forged. Here are key elements to cultivate effective silence in your meditation practice:

1. Physical Environment

Choose a Quiet Space: Begin by selecting a quiet and comfortable space for your meditation. Minimize external distractions to create an environment conducive to silence.

Comfortable Posture: Adopt a comfortable posture, whether sitting or lying down. Physical comfort is essential to allow the mind to settle without the distraction of discomfort.

2. Mindful Breathing:

Focus on the Breath: Bring your attention to the breath. The rhythmic nature of breathing serves as an anchor to the present moment. Notice the sensations of each inhale and exhale, allowing the breath to guide you into a state of calm.

Gentle Redirecting: When the mind wanders, gently

redirect your focus to the breath. This gentle redirection is a key component of effective silence, as it helps tame the constant chatter of the mind.

3. Inner Stillness

Let Go of Mental Noise: Silence in meditation is not just about external quietness; it involves letting go of mental noise. Allow thoughts to come and go without attaching to them. Cultivate an inner stillness by observing thoughts without judgment.

Embrace the Present Moment: Effective silence emerges when you fully embrace the present moment. Let go of concerns about the past or future. Center your awareness on the now, experiencing the richness of the present with an open heart.

4. Deepening Concentration

Single-Pointed Focus: Silence is amplified when you cultivate a single-pointed focus. Concentrate on a specific point of attention, whether it's the breath, a mantra, or a visual point. This focused attention deepens the meditative experience.

Progressive Deepening: As you settle into the meditation, notice the progressive deepening of silence. The mind becomes more tranquil, and the internal chatter diminishes, allowing you to enter a state of heightened awareness.

5. Extended Sessions

Lengthen Your Practice: Consider extending the duration of your meditation sessions gradually. Longer sessions provide more opportunities for the mind to settle into profound silence and for you to experience the transformative effects of sustained stillness.

Integration into Daily Life: Extend the benefits of

effective silence beyond formal meditation. Practice bringing moments of mindful silence into daily activities, such as mindful walking, eating, or simply being present in everyday tasks.

6. Reflection and Gratitude

Reflective Silence: Conclude your meditation with a few moments of reflective silence. Allow insights from the practice to naturally emerge. This reflective silence can deepen your understanding and appreciation of the meditation experience.

Gratitude for Silence: Cultivate a sense of gratitude for the moments of effective silence in your meditation. Recognize the value of these moments in fostering clarity, peace, and a deeper connection with yourself.

Effective silence in meditation is not a passive absence of noise; it is an active and intentional state cultivated through a combination of physical environment, mindful breathing, inner stillness, concentration, and extended practice. By incorporating these elements into your meditation routine, you create a space where the transformative power of silence can unfold, leading to a more profound and enriching meditation experience.

2. A - Affirmations

With the mind in a centered state, the next step involves affirmations. Affirmations are positive statements that articulate your goals, aspirations, and self-worth. By vocalizing these affirmations, you set a positive tone for the day, cultivating a mindset that aligns with your vision for personal growth and success. I still have my goal cards and affirmations in my journal and I read them daily, only it changes as per my requirements or on my current focal point.

Creating Effective Affirmations

Affirmations are potent tools that, when integrated into meditation, can profoundly influence the mind and enhance your overall well-being. Crafting effective affirmations involves choosing positive and empowering statements that align with your goals and aspirations. Here's how to creating and incorporating effective affirmations into your meditation practice:

1. **Positive and Present Tense:** Frame your affirmations in the present tense. Instead of saying, "I will be confident," state, "I am confident." This immediate, positive framing signals to the subconscious mind that the desired state is already unfolding.
2. **Personal and Specific:** Make affirmations personal and specific to your needs. Tailor them to address your unique goals and challenges. For example, if cultivating inner peace is a goal, affirm, "I am grounded and at peace in every moment."
3. **Concise and Clear:** Keep affirmations concise and clear. A brief, focused affirmation is easier to remember and internalize during meditation. Avoid lengthy statements and opt for words that carry emotional weight.
4. **Use Positive Language:** Frame affirmations in positive language. Instead of stating what you want to avoid, focus on what you want to attract. For instance, replace "I am not stressed" with "I am calm and centered."
5. **Present Emotionally Charged States:** Include emotional states in your affirmations. Infuse them with the feelings you want to experience. For instance, "I am filled with gratitude and joy" connects the affirmation to positive emotions.

6. **Repeat and Reinforce:** Repeat affirmations consistently during meditation. Repetition reinforces the message to the subconscious mind. Integrate affirmations into your breathing rhythm, repeating them with each inhale and exhale.
7. **Align with Core Values:** Ensure that your affirmations align with your core values and authentic self. Authenticity enhances the effectiveness of affirmations, as they resonate with your true aspirations.
8. **Visualize as You Affirm:** Combine visualization with affirmations. As you repeat the affirmation, visualize yourself embodying the qualities or achieving the goals described. This creates a multisensory experience that deepens the impact of the affirmation.
9. **Affirmations for Growth:** Craft affirmations that focus on growth and positive transformation. For example, "I am continuously evolving into the best version of myself" encapsulates the essence of personal development.
10. **Reflect on Affirmations:** After your meditation session, take a moment to reflect on the affirmations. Consider how they resonate with you and observe any shifts in your mindset. This reflection reinforces the integration of affirmations into your consciousness.
11. **Create Affirmation Themes:** Organize affirmations into themes based on areas of your life you want to nurture. For instance, have affirmations related to self-love, confidence, resilience, or gratitude. This thematic approach adds depth to your practice.
12. **Affirmations for the Present and the Future:** Blend affirmations that focus on the present with those

that envision future success. For example, "I am confident and capable in this moment, and my future is filled with abundance and success."

13. **Adapt Affirmations Over Time:** As your goals and aspirations evolve, adapt your affirmations accordingly. Regularly revisit and revise them to ensure they align with your current mindset and objectives.
14. **Embrace Positive Challenges:** Use affirmations to reframe challenges positively also known as pivoting. For instance, "I embrace challenges as opportunities for growth" shifts the perspective and encourages resilience.
15. **Affirmations as Statements of Gratitude:** Infuse gratitude into your affirmations. Express gratitude for present blessings and visualize future accomplishments with gratitude. Gratitude amplifies the positive energy of your affirmations.

Incorporating effective affirmations into your meditation practice enhances your ability to reshape thought patterns and manifest positive change. As you cultivate a habit of repeating affirmations with conviction and mindfulness, you create a powerful synergy between your conscious and subconscious mind, laying the foundation for personal growth and a more positive, fulfilling life.

3. V - Visualization

Visualization propels the S.A.V.E.R.S routine into the realm of imagination and creativity. Envisioning your goals and desired outcomes creates a mental blueprint for success. Visualization enhances motivation, helping you connect emotionally with your aspirations and instilling a sense of purpose in your actions.

The Transformative Power of Visualization in Meditation

Visualization, often referred to as guided imagery or mental rehearsal, is a potent technique that harnesses the mind's creative power during meditation. It involves creating vivid mental images to enhance relaxation, focus, and personal growth. Here's a comprehensive exploration of visualization in meditation, its process, importance, and how to effectively integrate it into your practice:

1. Process of Visualization in Meditation

Set the Stage: Begin your meditation session in a comfortable position. Close your eyes to shut out external stimuli, creating a mental canvas for visualization.

Relaxation: Engage in deep, calming breaths to promote relaxation. Let go of the tension in your body and allow your mind to settle.

Choose a Focus: Select a specific focal point for visualization. This could be a place, a scenario, or an object. It might be a serene beach, a lush forest, or a personal goal you want to achieve.

Vivid Imagery: Dive into the visualization with vivid imagery. Engage all your senses - see the colors, hear the sounds, feel the textures, and even smell the scents. Make the mental experience as immersive as possible.

Flow with the Narrative: Allow the visualization to unfold naturally. Whether it's a journey, an achievement, or a scene of tranquility, let the narrative progress without force, allowing your mind to guide the story.

Reflective Pause: Conclude the visualization with a reflective pause. Take a moment to absorb the feelings, insights, or inspiration that arose during the visualization.

2. Importance of Visualization in Meditation

Stress Reduction: Visualization promotes relaxation

by transporting the mind to calming and serene mental landscapes. This, in turn, helps reduce stress and anxiety.

Goal Manifestation: Visualization is a powerful tool for manifesting goals. By mentally rehearsing successful outcomes, you enhance your confidence and motivation to pursue those goals in reality.

Enhanced Focus and Concentration: Engaging in detailed visualizations sharpens your ability to concentrate. It trains your mind to sustain focus, a skill that extends beyond meditation into daily tasks.

Emotional Healing: Visualization can aid in emotional healing by allowing you to explore and process emotions in a safe mental space. It provides an avenue for releasing and transforming negative emotions.

3. How to Achieve Effective Visualization

Start Simple: If you're new to visualization, start with simple scenes or objects. As you become more comfortable, gradually progress to more complex visualizations.

Engage Multiple Senses: Incorporate multiple senses into your visualizations. The more senses you involve, the more immersive and impactful the experience becomes.

Personalize Your Visualization: Tailor visualizations to your personal preferences and goals. Whether it's a peaceful retreat or a goal achievement, make the imagery meaningful to you.

Practice Regularly: Like any skill, visualization improves with regular practice. Dedicate time to visualization in your meditation routine to strengthen this mental tool.

4. Incorporating Visualization into Daily Life

Mindful Breaks: Use brief visualizations during breaks in your day. Whether it's a work break or a moment of stress, take a few minutes to visualize a calming scene.

Preparation for Tasks: Before engaging in a challenging task or event, visualize a successful outcome. This primes your mind for success and enhances your performance.

Creative Problem Solving: Visualization can aid in creative problem-solving. Visualize different scenarios and potential solutions, allowing your mind to explore innovative possibilities.

5. Consistency and Patience

Consistent Practice: Integrate visualization into your meditation practice consistently. The benefits of visualization deepen with regular, dedicated sessions.

Be Patient with Progress: Visualization is a skill that develops over time. Be patient with yourself, and allow the process to unfold naturally. Celebrate the small victories along the way.

6. Benefits Beyond Meditation

Increased Confidence: Visualization cultivates a sense of confidence by mentally rehearsing success. This newfound confidence can positively impact your approach to various aspects of life.

Creative Inspiration: Visualization stimulates creativity by allowing your mind to explore different images, scenarios, and possibilities. It can be a valuable tool for creative individuals seeking inspiration.

Positive Mindset: Regular engagement in positive visualizations contributes to the development of a positive mindset. This optimistic outlook can influence your perception of challenges and opportunities.

Visualization in meditation is a dynamic and transformative practice that engages the mind's creative capacity. By incorporating vivid imagery into your meditation routine with consistency and intention, you unlock the potential for stress reduction, goal manifestation, enhanced focus, and emotional healing. Visualization is not just a meditation technique; it is a gateway to unlocking the mind's incredible power for personal growth and well-being.

4. E - Exercise

Physical well-being is a cornerstone of personal development. The "E" in S.A.V.E.R.S stands for exercise, advocating for the inclusion of physical activity in your morning routine. Whether it's a brisk walk, yoga, or a full workout, incorporating exercise boosts energy levels, improves mood, and enhances overall health, setting a positive tone for the day ahead.

Exercise has a multitude of positive effects on both the body and the mind. Regular physical activity is associated with numerous health benefits, contributing to overall well-being. Here are some key effects of exercise:

Physical Effects

1. **Improved Cardiovascular Health:** Regular exercise strengthens the heart and improves circulation. It helps lower blood pressure, reduce the risk of heart disease, and enhance overall cardiovascular health.
2. **Weight Management:** Exercise plays a crucial role in weight management by burning calories and increasing metabolism. It helps in both weight loss and maintaining a healthy weight.
3. **Muscle Strength and Endurance:** Resistance training and aerobic exercise contribute to the development of muscle strength and endurance. Strong muscles support joint health and improve overall functional capacity.
4. **Enhanced Flexibility and Balance:** Activities like yoga and stretching exercises improve flexibility and

balance. This can reduce the risk of falls, especially in older adults.

5. **Bone Health:** Weight-bearing exercises, such as walking and strength training, contribute to bone health. They help maintain bone density and reduce the risk of osteoporosis.
6. **Improved Immune Function:** Moderate, regular exercise is associated with a strengthened immune system. It may reduce the risk of chronic diseases and enhance the body's ability to fight off infections.
7. **Better Sleep Quality:** Regular physical activity is linked to improved sleep quality. It helps regulate sleep patterns and contributes to a more restful night's sleep.
8. **Joint Health:** Exercise helps maintain joint health by promoting proper lubrication and reducing stiffness. It is beneficial for individuals with arthritis and other joint-related conditions.

Mental and Emotional Effects

1. **Mood Enhancement:** Exercise stimulates the release of endorphins, the body's natural mood lifters. It can help alleviate symptoms of depression and anxiety and promote a sense of well-being.
2. **Stress Reduction:** Physical activity acts as a stress reliever by reducing levels of stress hormones like cortisol. Engaging in exercise provides a healthy outlet for managing stress.
3. **Improved Cognitive Function:** Regular exercise has been associated with improved cognitive function, including better memory, attention, and executive function. It may also reduce the risk of cognitive decline with aging.
4. **Increased Energy Levels:** Exercise improves overall

energy levels and reduces feelings of fatigue. It enhances the efficiency of the cardiovascular and respiratory systems, leading to increased stamina.

5. **Enhanced Self-Esteem and Body Image:** Achieving fitness goals through exercise can boost self-esteem and body image. Engaging in physical activity provides a sense of accomplishment and empowerment.
6. **Social Interaction:** Group exercise activities or team sports provide opportunities for social interaction, fostering a sense of community and support. Social connections contribute to mental well-being.
7. **Anxiety Reduction:** Regular exercise has anxiolytic effects, helping to reduce symptoms of anxiety. It promotes relaxation and a sense of control over one's body and mind.
8. **Increased Brain Plasticity:** Physical activity has been associated with increased brain plasticity, which is the brain's ability to reorganize itself and adapt to new experiences and information.

Long-Term Health Benefits

1. **Disease Prevention:** Regular exercise is a key factor in preventing chronic diseases such as cardiovascular disease, type 2 diabetes, certain cancers, and metabolic syndrome.
2. **Longevity:** Engaging in regular physical activity is linked to increased life expectancy. It contributes to overall health, reducing the risk of premature mortality.
3. **Improved Quality of Life:** The combination of physical, mental, and emotional benefits contributes to an improved overall quality of life. Regular exercise is associated with a more active and fulfilling lifestyle.

The effects of exercise extend beyond physical fitness, impacting mental health, emotional well-being, and long-term health outcomes. Incorporating regular physical activity into your routine can contribute to a healthier, more vibrant life.

5. R - Reading

Knowledge is a potent catalyst for personal transformation. Reading forms the "R" in S.A.V.E.R.S, encouraging a daily commitment to acquiring new insights. Whether it's self-help books, educational material, or inspirational literature, dedicating time to reading stimulates intellectual growth and broadens your perspective.

Reading has a profound impact on various aspects of cognitive, emotional, and social well-being. Here are some key effects of reading:

Cognitive Effects

1. **Enhanced Knowledge and Learning:** Reading exposes individuals to a wide range of information, ideas, and perspectives. It is a primary means of acquiring knowledge and expanding one's understanding of the world.
2. **Improved Vocabulary:** Regular reading contributes to the development of a rich and varied vocabulary. Exposure to diverse written material exposes readers to new words and expressions.
3. **Cognitive Stimulation:** Reading engages the brain in a mentally stimulating activity. It requires focus, concentration, and the ability to comprehend complex ideas, contributing to overall cognitive function.
4. **Critical Thinking Skills:** Reading encourages critical thinking and analysis. Engaging with different genres and styles of writing prompts

readers to evaluate information, form opinions, and make informed decisions.

5. **Enhanced Memory:** Reading, especially challenging material, stimulates the brain and can improve memory retention. It requires the brain to remember characters, plot details, and other elements of the story.
6. **Improved Focus and Concentration:** Regular reading helps improve focus and concentration. The act of immersing oneself in a book requires sustained attention, training the mind to concentrate for extended periods.

Emotional Effects

1. **Stress Reduction:** Reading, particularly fiction, can provide an escape from daily stressors. Engaging with a captivating story allows readers to temporarily disconnect and relax.
2. **Empathy and Emotional Intelligence:** Fictional literature, in particular, allows readers to empathize with characters and understand diverse perspectives. This emotional engagement contributes to the development of empathy and emotional intelligence.
3. **Mood Regulation:** Reading can have a positive impact on mood regulation. Inspirational or uplifting material can boost mood, while literature that explores complex emotions can help readers process their own feelings.
4. **Purification:** Reading provides a safe space for emotional catharsis. Readers may find solace, understanding, or a sense of connection with characters going through similar challenges.
5. **Increased Self-Awareness:** Reading self-help or reflective literature can contribute to increased self-

awareness. Insights from books can prompt readers to reflect on their own experiences, thoughts, and emotions.

Social Effects

1. **Increased Empathy:** Exposure to diverse characters and situations in literature fosters empathy. Readers gain insights into the lives of others, promoting a deeper understanding of different cultures and perspectives.
2. **Connection and Community:** Shared reading experiences can foster a sense of community. Book clubs, discussions, and online forums provide opportunities for readers to connect, share insights, and engage in meaningful conversations.
3. **Cultural Awareness:** Reading literature from different cultures enhances cultural awareness. It exposes readers to diverse traditions, histories, and societal norms, promoting a more inclusive worldview.
4. **Communication Skills:** Regular reading contributes to the development of effective communication skills. Exposure to well-written language models proper grammar, syntax, and communication styles.
5. **Inspiration for Creativity:** Reading can inspire creativity. Exposure to different writing styles, genres, and imaginative storytelling can spark creative thinking and contribute to one's own creative endeavors.
6. **Social Bonds:** Shared reading experiences, whether within families, classrooms, or social groups, can strengthen social bonds. Discussing books and sharing stories creates connections between individuals.

In summary, reading has a multifaceted impact on cognitive abilities, emotional well-being, and social connections. Whether for education, relaxation, or personal growth, the act of reading contributes to a richer, more fulfilling life.

6. S - Scribing (Journaling)

The final pillar of the S.A.V.E.R.S routine is scribing, or journaling. Documenting your thoughts, feelings, and goals provides a reflective space. Journaling can take various forms, from gratitude journaling to goal-setting, allowing you to track progress, gain insights, and cultivate self-awareness.

Journaling offers a wide range of benefits for mental, emotional, and even physical well-being. Some key advantages of incorporating journaling into your routine:

1. **Self-Reflection and Self-Awareness:** Journaling provides a space for introspection, allowing you to explore your thoughts, emotions, and experiences. This process fosters self-awareness, helping you understand yourself on a deeper level.
2. **Stress Reduction:** Writing in a journal can be a therapeutic way to release pent-up emotions and manage stress. It offers a healthy outlet for expressing concerns, fears, and frustrations.
3. **Emotional Regulation:** By putting your feelings into words, you gain a better understanding of your emotions. This clarity can contribute to improved emotional regulation and a greater sense of control.
4. **Problem Solving:** Journaling encourages you to analyze challenges, explore potential solutions, and gain perspective on issues. It can be a valuable tool for problem-solving and decision-making.
5. **Enhanced Creativity:** Engaging in creative writing,

doodling, or other artistic expressions in your journal can stimulate creativity. It provides an outlet for imagination and innovative thinking.

6. **Improved Communication Skills:** Regular journaling can enhance your written communication skills. It allows you to practice articulating your thoughts, ideas, and feelings, contributing to clearer expression.
7. **Goal Setting and Achievement:** Journaling provides a structured way to set and track goals. Writing down aspirations, breaking them into actionable steps, and reflecting on progress can boost motivation and achievement.
8. **Positive Affirmation and Gratitude:** Incorporating positive affirmations and gratitude into your journaling practice can cultivate a positive mindset. Focusing on what you're thankful for promotes a sense of well-being.

Journaling comes in various forms, each catering to different preferences, needs, and creative expressions. Types of journaling that you might find interesting:

1. **Traditional Journaling:** The classic pen-and-paper approach involves writing daily entries, reflections, and thoughts in a physical journal. Offers a tangible, personal connection to your thoughts. The act of physical writing can be therapeutic.
2. **Digital Journaling:** Journaling using digital platforms, apps, or online platforms. Provides accessibility and the ability to organize, search, and sync entries across devices. Some apps offer features like multimedia integration and prompts.
3. **Bullet Journaling:** A structured method of journaling that uses bullet points, symbols, and short phrases

to organize tasks, events, and thoughts. Excellent for organization, goal setting, and task management. Allows for quick and efficient note-taking.

4. **Art Journaling:** Combines written expression with artistic elements like drawings, paintings, collages, and other visual mediums. Fosters creativity, self-expression, and provides an outlet for artistic exploration.
5. **Gratitude Journaling:** Focuses specifically on recording things you're grateful for each day. Encourages a positive mindset, helps shift focus to positive aspects of life, and promotes feelings of gratitude.
6. **Travel Journaling:** Documents experiences, observations, and feelings while traveling. Creates lasting memories, allows for reflection on cultural experiences, and serves as a travel keepsake.
7. **Dream Journaling:** Records dreams and interpretations upon waking. Can help improve dream recall, explore the subconscious, and provide insights into emotions and concerns.
8. **Mindfulness Journaling:** Focuses on the present moment, incorporating observations, sensations, and reflections on mindfulness practices. Enhances self-awareness, deepens mindfulness practices, and promotes a sense of presence.
9. **Morning Pages:** Popularized by Julia Cameron, involves writing three pages of stream-of-consciousness thoughts every morning. Clears the mind, overcomes creative blocks, and serves as a tool for self-discovery.
10. **Five-Minute Journaling:** A structured journaling format with prompts encouraging you to reflect

on positive aspects, set intentions, and express gratitude. Quick and easy, promotes a positive mindset, and sets a positive tone for the day.

11. **Reflective Journaling:** Involves thoughtful reflection on experiences, personal growth, and life events. Supports self-discovery, provides a space for contemplation, and aids in processing emotions.
12. **Idea Journaling:** Captures creative ideas, brainstorming, and innovative thoughts. Fosters creativity provides a repository for inspiration, and helps in project planning.
13. **Reading Journal:** Documents thoughts, reactions, and reflections on books you've read. Enhances comprehension, deepens engagement with literature, and creates a personal reading record.
14. **Fitness Journal:** Tracks workouts, nutrition, and overall fitness progress. Enhances accountability, allows for goal setting, and provides insights into health and wellness.
15. **One-Sentence Journaling:** Records a single sentence summarizing the day's highlights or reflections. Quick and efficient, captures key moments, and encourages regular journaling.
16. **Themed Journaling:** Focuses on specific themes or topics, such as relationships, career, or personal development. Provides a structured approach to explore and deepen understanding in specific areas of life.
17. **Letter Journaling:** Writing letters to yourself, others, or even fictional characters. Offers a unique form of self-expression, helps process emotions, and serves as a creative outlet.

Experimenting with different forms of journaling can

help you discover the style that resonates most with you. Whether you prefer written entries, visual expression, or a combination of both, journaling is a versatile practice that can be tailored to your individual preferences and goals.

Sample Morning Routine incorporating S.A.V.E.R.S

Silence (5 minutes):

Practice deep breathing or mindfulness meditation.

Affirmations (5 minutes):

Repeat personalized affirmations that align with your restart goals.

Visualization (5 minutes):

Visualize yourself successfully navigating your new chapter in life.

Exercise (15 minutes):

Engage in a workout, yoga, or a brisk morning walk.

Reading (10 minutes):

Read a motivational book or articles related to your goals.

Scribing (Journaling) (10 minutes):

Write about your goals, reflections, and any insights gained.

Adapting the S.A.V.E.R.S routine to your specific needs and goals can contribute to a positive and proactive mindset as you navigate restarting your life after a break. Consistent practice can help you build resilience, clarity, and a strong foundation for your journey ahead.

Embracing S.A.V.E.R.S as a Lifestyle

The S.A.V.E.R.S routine is not just a collection of practices; it is a lifestyle choice. By dedicating intentional time each morning to these transformative activities, individuals can lay the groundwork for sustained personal development.

Routine promotes mindfulness, self-discovery, and the cultivation of habits that contribute to a more fulfilling and purpose-driven life.

The S.A.V.E.R.S morning routine serves as a roadmap for personal growth and holistic well-being. By investing time and energy in each element, individuals embark on a journey of self-discovery, setting the stage for a day filled with intention, positivity, and transformative potential.

15

(A) The 3p Blueprint

"One can have no smaller or greater mastery than mastery of oneself."
– Leonardo da Vinci

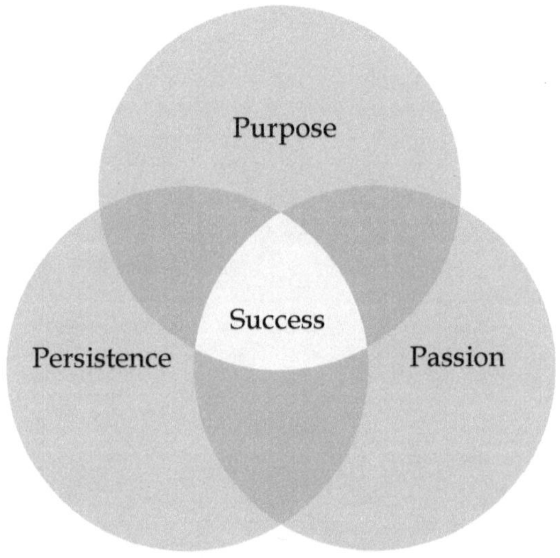

The 3P blueprint, often associated with women's empowerment, typically refers to Passion, Perseverance and Persistence. Understanding and embodying the 3P blueprint can be highly beneficial for women in various aspects of their personal and professional lives. Here's why it is important:

Passion

Passion plays a significant role in the lives of women, just as it does for everyone else. Passion is essential in the lives of women as it contributes to personal fulfillment, career success, empowerment, community engagement, and overall well-being. By embracing their passions and pursuing their dreams, women can lead more meaningful and impactful lives, while also inspiring others to do the same.

Career Success: Women who are passionate about their work are often more driven and motivated to excel in their careers. Passion fuels ambition, creativity, and innovation, leading to greater professional success and fulfillment.

Empowerment: When women follow their passions, they feel empowered to take control of their lives and make choices that align with their values and interests. This empowerment can have a ripple effect, influencing other areas of their lives and contributing to their overall well-being.

Breaking Gender Stereotypes: Pursuing passions that may traditionally be seen as "male-dominated" can challenge gender stereotypes and inspire other women to do the same. By defying societal expectations, women can pave the way for greater gender equality and representation in various fields.

Health and Well-being: Engaging in activities that ignite passion can have positive effects on women's mental and emotional well-being. Passionate pursuits provide a sense of purpose, reduce stress, and increase overall happiness and life satisfaction.

Perseverance

Perseverance is crucial in the lives of all individuals, regardless of gender. However, in the context of women's lives, perseverance can hold particular significance due to historical and societal factors. perseverance is of utmost importance in women's lives as it empowers them to overcome obstacles, achieve their goals, challenge stereotypes, and drive positive change in society. It is a powerful tool for personal growth, empowerment, and advancement, enabling women to fulfill their potential and make a meaningful impact in the world

Breaking Barriers: Historically, women have faced numerous barriers and discrimination in various aspects of life, including education, employment, and leadership positions. Perseverance allows women to break through these barriers, persisting despite obstacles and societal expectations.

Achieving Goals: Perseverance is essential for women to pursue and achieve their goals, whether they are personal, professional, or academic. It involves staying focused, determined, and resilient in the face of challenges and setbacks.

Overcoming Stereotypes: In many societies, women are often subjected to stereotypes and biases that undermine their abilities and potential. Perseverance enables women to challenge these stereotypes by demonstrating their capabilities through hard work, dedication, and resilience.

Creating Change: Perseverance plays a vital role in driving social and cultural change. Women who persevere in challenging norms, advocating for gender equality, and fighting injustice contribute to the progress of society as a whole.

Persistence

Persistence is a cornerstone of success for everyone, and its importance in the lives of women cannot be overstated. Persistence is essential in the lives of women as it empowers them to overcome obstacles, achieve their goals, advocate for change, and inspire others. It is a fundamental attribute that contributes to personal and professional success, as well as the advancement of gender equality and social justice.

Breaking through Societal Norms: Women often face societal norms and expectations that may discourage them from pursuing their ambitions or expressing their opinions. Persistence allows women to push through these barriers, challenging stereotypes and paving the way for gender equality.

Education and Skill Development: Persistence is essential for women pursuing education and skill development. In many parts of the world, girls and women still face barriers to accessing quality education. By persistently pursuing their academic goals, women can acquire the knowledge and skills needed to succeed in their chosen fields.

Advocacy and Activism: Many women are passionate advocates for social justice, gender equality, and women's rights. Persistence is crucial in driving meaningful change in these areas. By persistently speaking out, organizing movements, and advocating for policy change, women can make a significant impact on society.

Personal Growth and Resilience: On a personal level, persistence fosters resilience and growth. It allows women to bounce back from failures and setbacks, learn from their experiences, and continue moving forward with determination and resilience.

Understanding and embodying the 3P blueprint can empower women to navigate their personal and professional lives with confidence, purpose, and fulfillment. By recognizing their power, aligning with their purpose, and infusing passion into their pursuits, women can contribute to a more empowered and inclusive society.

(B) Boss Babes: Navigating the corporate comeback

How employers and corporates can accommodate women returnees and the steps need to be taken.

As women decide to return after a career hiatus they are plagued with a series of self-doubts like, will their profile even get shortlisted, are their skills outdated in the evolving job market, will they be able to balance work and home, will they be able to match to the expectations at work. Their emotional readiness is being tested at this stage. It is very critical for women to have self-confidence, anchored by emotional and physical support from her family during this time. Women who are able to create a robust support system around them are in a better spot to return.

Also, in terms of industry competitiveness, they might be on a backfoot as their skills might not be considered relevant with evolving technology and dynamic work environment. It is always recommended that women stay in touch with their area of work and make efforts towards honing their skills during the career break.

There are many other important external factors like lack of policies around flexi working, travel time and the sharp decline in income that women suffer after childbirth, often termed as motherhood penalty impacting the decision to return from a career break. Women face several challenges when returning to work after giving birth.

Challenges and Common problems shared by women

Lack of Supportive Policies: Many workplaces do not have adequate policies and support systems in place for new mothers. This includes insufficient maternity leave, lack of flexible work arrangements, and limited childcare facilities near the workplace.

Balancing Work and Family: Juggling the demands of work and caring for a newborn can be overwhelming. Women often struggle to find a balance between their professional responsibilities and the needs of their child, which can lead to increased stress and guilt.

Breastfeeding and Pumping Challenges: For women who choose to breastfeed, returning to work can pose challenges. Finding suitable spaces and time for pumping breast milk can be difficult, especially in workplaces that lack designated lactation rooms or supportive policies.

Career Progression: Taking time off for maternity leave can impact a woman's career progression. Women may feel disadvantaged compared to their peers who did not take a break, and they may face difficulties in catching up or regaining lost opportunities.

Discrimination and Bias: Women may experience discrimination or bias upon returning to work. This can manifest in various ways, such as being overlooked for promotions or being assigned fewer challenging tasks due to assumptions about their commitment or productivity after becoming a mother.

Emotional and Mental Well-being: Postpartum challenges, such as hormonal changes, sleep deprivation, and adjusting to the demands of motherhood, can affect a woman's emotional and mental well-being. Returning to work in this state can exacerbate stress and lead to feelings of overwhelm and exhaustion.

Limited Career Support: Some women may lack access to career development programs, mentoring, or networking opportunities that could help them navigate their return to work successfully. This lack of support can hinder their professional growth and advancement.

It's important for employers to recognize and address these challenges by implementing family-friendly policies, offering flexible work arrangements, providing adequate maternity leave, creating supportive environments, and promoting a culture of inclusivity and equal opportunities for women.

But a little planning and effort during the career break can play its part in reducing the apprehensions and fears which the word 'career break' brings in the minds of returning women and even recruiters at the time of selection.

Solutions for the challenges women face when returning to work

Flexible Work Arrangements: Employers can offer flexible work schedules, such as part-time or remote work options, to help women balance their work and family responsibilities more effectively. This flexibility allows them to adjust their work hours or location based on their child's needs.

Extended Maternity Leave: Providing longer maternity leave periods allows women to have sufficient time to recover from childbirth, bond with their newborn, and adjust to their new role as a mother. Longer leave periods also facilitate a smoother transition back to work.

Supportive Policies: Employers should establish supportive policies that specifically address the needs of working mothers. This includes policies that support breastfeeding, such as providing designated lactation rooms, flexible break times for pumping, and support for milk storage.

Childcare Facilities: Employers can consider providing on-site or nearby childcare facilities to ease the burden of finding suitable and reliable childcare. This enables women to have peace of mind while at work, knowing that their child is in a safe and nurturing environment.

Career Development Programs: Offering career development programs and opportunities for women returning to work after giving birth is crucial. This includes mentoring programs, training sessions, and networking events to help women regain momentum in their careers and stay updated with industry advancements.

Addressing Discrimination and Bias: Employers should actively work to eliminate discrimination and bias against working mothers. This includes implementing policies and training programs to ensure fair treatment, equal opportunities, and protection against discrimination based on pregnancy or caregiving responsibilities.

Employee Assistance Programs: Providing access to employee assistance programs that offer counseling, support, and resources for emotional well-being can help women manage the stress and challenges associated with returning to work after giving birth.

Employee Resource Groups: Establishing employee resource groups focused on supporting working parents, including working mothers, creates a sense of community and provides a platform for sharing experiences, advice, and resources.

Transparent Communication: Employers should foster

open and transparent communication with employees about their rights, benefits, and resources available to them as working parents. Clear communication helps women understand their options and feel supported throughout their transition.

Work-Life Integration: Promote a culture that values work-life integration rather than strict separation. Encourage boundaries between work and personal life, provide opportunities for flexible scheduling, and support work-life balance initiatives for all employees.

By implementing these solutions, employers can create a more supportive and inclusive work environment also consideration of these few things will enable women to successfully navigate their return to work after giving birth while maintaining a healthy work-life balance also promotes their professional development and success. Recognizing the unique challenges faced by this group and implementing supportive policies and programs will contribute to building a more diverse and inclusive workforce

For many new women employees, the relationship with their boss is critical to engagement and job satisfaction. Having my own experience as a bitter reminder of this and as a leader in order to have a solution I felt the need to understand the reason for this gap and set out to explore this relationship. The generational groups share some common values and beliefs: both workers and their bosses feel that patience, appreciation, psychological safety, and flexibility are key to cultivating good professional relationships and staying engaged in their work.

Differences between genders

I have felt there are five differences that stand out between genders and represent potential areas for tension. Differences emerged in their perspectives on:

1. **Empathy:** While women ranked empathy as their second most important trait in a boss, most bosses placed it a distant fifth. For women, empathy is a prerequisite for taking on more responsibility and increasing engagement. Bosses who struggle to be more empathetic with their employees run the risk of disengagement, leading to lost productivity and increased turnover. By focusing on respect and showing curiosity about what would help them feel more engaged, rather than productivity measures and tangible outcomes, bosses can help women feel more valued.
2. **Mental health:** Women workers feel they are not getting the mental health support they need, and they believe their ideas on the mental health impacts of work differ from those of their bosses. This situation is heightened by a hybrid work environment when employees working from home may find it challenging to maintain a healthy workload. Bosses can make a focused effort to "keep an eye on" the mental health of their employees and create opportunities for connection.
3. **Work and personal identity:** Women workers and their bosses differ in how important they view work as a part of their personal identities. 61% of Women in the workplace say their work is important to their identity, compared with 86% of their bosses. While entering the workforce is always a transitional period, it has been particularly difficult for Women, perhaps due to their purpose-driven nature or the blurred lines between work and home. Bosses may need to seek opportunities to get to know Women better and learn more about their priorities, identity, and values, then rethink how they motivate employees. Women may learn that engaging in the

workplace can help them grow and evolve their personal identity.

4. **Training and job readiness:** In an increasingly hybrid world, Women workers and their bosses alike recognize a deficiency in training and development that would prepare them for their jobs. To address this gap, bosses and their organizations need to improve these programs and engage Women in using their energy and problem-solving skills to enhance the effectiveness of their workforce and to lower the potential for turnover. The potential benefit? Women who are learning the skills they need for the future in their jobs are 2.5x times more likely to stay at their current organization.
5. **Reward and recognition:** Women want greater flexibility and time off as a reward for working long hours and meeting deadlines, while bosses favor more traditional forms of reward and recognition. Younger workers are looking for a chance to recharge, reconnect, and pursue their personal passions after a time of intense work. While bosses may have organizational or attitudinal constraints around time off, there's an opportunity for the generations to align on using time off as a reward to help increase positive engagement.

How can we bridge the gender gap

Women bosses did agree on one area; the workplace can and must change. Bosses expressed optimism about exploring and developing solutions: More than seven in ten bosses said they are excited about the ways that the workplace will change as Women makes up an increasingly greater portion of it. The first step is identifying the challenges and understanding why they exist. What remains to be seen is how we all work together to shape the workforce of the future.

I realized at the age of 35 that I was a person who:

Sought comfort in every aspect of life

Scared change on uncertainty

Avoided situations that made me uncomfortable

Felt under confident and fragile

Little did I know that every aversion to discomfort was actually accelerating my personal growth. Did I change? Yes, I decided to face my fears one by one and challenged myself to explore the unknown.

I did fail and quit, but I remained steadfast. Today, I am confident enough to move out of my comfort zone, trying new things exploring the unknown world and moving in the direction where life is taking me. I have decided to create an impact on the world and help others in every small way I can to anyone who feels the need of help to get up and rebuild. What I am today is a combination of trials and errors and effort and support of my partner, kids, family, and friends.

I decided to start the journey of a change maker to help others see their paths and build a community safe for them to discuss their confusions or seek guidance.

To all those working professionals do not get exhausted, you are capable of so much more than you believe!!

To all those who feel stuck in life, who don't know where to start again and realize your true protentional.

I set out on a journey to build again, did not know how, to be true I was not equipped for this reroute of life. The next step seemed like focusing on what, why and how. For this I had to go deep and get to know exactly what is that I am creating. One more thing which attracted this to me was I wanted to create a stronger and unshakable me, whom no situation, no emotion can weaken. The law of attraction is not new to us, I liked it because it gave me a structured process. Approaching things systematically helps me to be focused.

(C) Getting Ready for the change

Taking a break to nurture family or any other responsibility is a choice many women make. How ever, it's time to burst the myth that returning to work is impossible or such women. With the right approach, they can get back to having a great career.

My two steps that started the preparations was:

1. Begin your journey by journaling, determine your skills, strengths and interests. What kind of work are you passionate about? As per your skills and situation what kind of job do you prefer.
2. Create resume tailored to your skill set. you can use various online resources, like Canva or Microsoft, to select a suitable resume template and build a professional resume.

Here, I am listing the steps that helped me get on track and prevent feelings of overwhelm. The plan below

helped me stay focused and consistent. Allocate two hours every day to complete at least two tasks from the list below

Research and Goal setting: Research industries and job roles, identify potential employers or companies you want to work for on LinkedIn and reach out to them.

- **Networking:** Connect with former colleagues on LinkedIn. Attend networking events. Reach out to friends and acquaintances in your field.
- **Resume and Cover Letter:** Update your resume with your most recent skills and experiences. Create a compelling cover letter template.
- **Online presence:** Enhance your LinkedIn profile and share relevant articles and posts to demonstrate your expertise.
- **Connect with recruiters:** Reach out to recruitment agencies specializing in your industry. Submit your resume to job search websites.
- **Online courses and skill enhancement:** Identify skills that need improving and enrol in online courses or workshops.
- **Practice answering interview questions:** prepare and practice mock interview to elevate your pitch.
- **Keep a record for job application and follow-ups:** Maintain an excel file for the same.
- **Follow up and review:** reflect on your progress and adapt your strategy is needed.
- **Seek mentorship:** seeking help is not a sign of weakness, so take help as and when required.

Sincere effort and hard work will definitely pay off if done being aligned and in connection with your higher conscious makes the journey much easier and fruitful.

(D) Pump up your power with Reinventing work sheet

Make a list of all the elements of your identity you want to have in each area of your life you want to change: As you make the list, write all the power you have right now and all that you decide to change. Identify individuals who possess the qualities you aspire to adopt.. Make note of all the changes you need to make to be that character.

....

....

....

Expand your imagination and consciously choose and describe each change in detail, get excited as a kid and go into details.

....

....

....

Develop a plan of action you could take that would cause you to know that you are truly living consistently with your new identity.

....

....

....

www.ingramcontent.com/pod-product-compliance
Lightning Source LLC
LaVergne TN
LVHW091130080826
845145LV00008B/2110

* 9 7 8 8 1 9 6 9 2 0 9 7 5 *